Praise For the C

The Compassion Code serves as a valuable guide to help us navigate difficult emotional events in our own lives, as well as in the lives of others. Laura's practical approach to a difficult subject is not only easy to read, but is also an important resource which I know I will refer to often. ~**Sharon Hymes, MD**

As a deeply compassionate, loving, open, and accepting person, Laura is the best person I know to teach people how to be the friends, family members, and compassionate colleagues we all hope we'll be in times of crisis for our loved ones. The Compassion Code is a how to guide not just on what to say when life goes wrong—but a guide on how to live life itself. I'm proud to have Laura as a friend, and I know this book's impact will be felt around the world. ~**Kaneisha Grayson, Founder of The Art of Applying and Author of *Be Your Own Boyfriend***

If you read, internalize, and live by the principles and practices Laura so beautifully gifts us in The Compassion Code, your relationships with others—and with yourself—will improve dramatically and you will see benefits beyond what you could have imagined. I will use this readable, enjoyable and relatable resource often in my personal and professional life and I would recommend it to anyone would could use a little more compassion in his or her life. That being all of us, I would recommend it to everyone.

~**Mor Regev, LMSW**

Truly one of the most beautiful books I have ever read. And one of the most world changing. How many wars could have been avoided if we all just had the skill of knowing what to say when emotions run high and fear, grief and anger are in the room. Laura Jack weaves a simple and elegant framework for creating amazing possibility in the midst of massive breakdown.

~**Teresa de Grosbois #1 Bestselling author of *Mass Influence***

Reading The Compassion Code is like talking to a wise best friend who can guide you through so many aspects of life, especially those dark or confusing times. Thanks to Laura, I've banned the phrase "I'm fine," in my life and have so many more tools for connecting with the people I love.
~**Suzanne Boothby, author of *The After Cancer Diet***

Oh, how I want everyone to read this book! Laura Jack has written this gem with remarkable sensitivity, kindness, and brilliance, and I honestly believe that every person could learn and grow with immense positivity from reading it. Even the most compassionate of people will take away something of value; the rest will have a new perspective they will surely be grateful for. The Compassion Code touched me in a way that no other book has, and I believe it will do the same for every reader who embraces its pages of love and wisdom."

~Stacey Aaronson, publishing partner and founder of The Book Doctor Is In

Laura Jack is the real deal... she understands the realities of coping with loss and change in a way that supports emotional wellness, personal growth and transformation. The Compassion Code is an important read for care givers, and those wanting to know how to best support their friends, family and colleagues who are experiencing change and loss. **~Charmaine Hammond, professional speaker and best selling author**

The Compassion Code should be mandatory reading for every human being. We all experience challenging emotions at different points in our lives, yet many of us don't know what to say or do when someone is suffering, or even know how to take care of ourselves when we're suffering. The Compassion Code breaks down these common, yet often hidden, aspects of our human experience and offers practical guidance on how to better support, connect with, and love others and ourselves.

~Jackie Vecchio, Writer at Create Happy

This book touches on themes much more expansive than just compassion. It's about growth, healing, challenging unhelpful thoughts and connecting. This book taps into parts of ourselves that we're either not paying attention to, or don't even know are there, but are definitely important to explore. And she gives tangible suggestions throughout the book that are approachable and impactful. Laura Jack is a voice that is not going anywhere. And good thing for that.

~Daniel Saxe, Founder of OfertaSimple.com

For anyone who has ever wondered what to say in a difficult situation, this book is for you. Laura has mastered the art of compassionate communication and now brings it to you in this amazing book!

~Heather Jernigan, Creative Marketing Director and Business Coach

THE COMPASSION CODE

How to say the right thing when the wrong thing happens

LAURA JACK

KAT BIGGIE PRESS
COLUMBIA, SC, USA

Published by Kat Biggie Press.
Columbia, SC 29229
http://katbiggiepress.com

Cover Design: Samantha Paris Estes and Michelle Fairbanks
Interior Design: Write.Publish.Sell
Editing: Stacey Aaronson
Author Photo Credit: Abbey Corbett Photography

ISBN 978-0-9987779-4-8
Library of Congress Control Number: 2017948444
First Edition: August 2017

10 9 8 7 6 5 4 3 2 1

Dedication

To my mamasita and my daughter, Ayla.

Contents

Dear Compassionate Warrior,

Does it ever feel like you have a sign across your head that says, "Tell me your troubles"?

You know who you are. You are the front line for humanity, the compassionate undercover caregivers. You work with people daily, either professionally or personally, and you support them through their troubles.

I can relate. Whether I ask or not, people tend to tell me their stories, and I love hearing them. I love learning about their relationships, their hopes and dreams, and even their losses.

If you are a human, and you have a story (you do), then I am interested in knowing it. What I have come to realize, and why I am writing this book, is that we don't always know what to say when people share the challenging stories of their lives, and sometimes we even say the wrong things in response. Often we become drained by other people's stories because we think we have to have all the answers, which often leads us to stop asking the questions.

Let me start by saying thank you. Thank you for being on the front lines. I know it's not always easy.

Thank you for caring enough to ask, and more importantly, for caring enough to listen to the answer. We need more people like you on the planet.

With deep gratitude and love,

Laura

Foreword

Compassion is simultaneously one of the most important aspects of being human and also the trickiest. Without compassion, we are left to live in a world that feels lonely, isolating, and cold. But, with too much compassion, we find ourselves over-sacrificing and over-giving at the expense of ourselves.

Laura Jack has taken over a decade of knowledge, study, and lived wisdom and created a timeless manual for mastering the art of compassion and living from our hearts. When I first read The Compassion Code, something deep inside of me shifted. It changed the way I see myself. It changed the way I view the world. It catalyzed a new way of how I show up in my relationships, in my business, and with myself.

The truth is that a similar awakening happened in me when I first met Laura. If you ever have the opportunity to meet her, you'll know exactly what I'm talking about. The moment I hugged Laura, I knew we would be soul sisters for life.

Over the course of our friendship, Laura and I have built businesses together, spent hours in deep conversation, texted when in crisis and when in celebration, and generally become best friends. We've coached each other through challenges, loved each other through loss, and held each other in tears and laughter. Laura has taught me what it means to be a friend—and she has ushered me into a new way of living, with compassion as my compass.

Laura handed me *The Compassion Code* at a perfect time. I had just found out I was pregnant, so I was in the "in between" phase of simultaneously feeling joy and also mourning the loss of my old life as I knew it. As Laura so perfectly describes in this book, any loss or change of state is a grieving experience. Halfway through reading this profound book, in the midst of my joy and grief over being pregnant, I had a miscarriage. My initial grief of losing my former life turned into the grief of mourning the loss of my future life.

This book—and Laura Jack's wisdom—saved me. I learned that grief shows up in many different ways. Things I used to call "depression" or "anger," Laura simply refers to as one of the many faces of grief. What I have learned from Laura, and what you will find in this book, is that in order to have true compassion for others, we must first have compassion for ourselves. Yet, the only way we can ever have compassion for ourselves is if we give ourselves full permission to feel it all.

The Compassion Code provides one breakthrough after another. You know those books that fill you with something inexplicable from the moment you pick them up? Well, you have in your hands one of those books. Through every page, every story, and every inquiry, you can feel Laura's love, tenderness, and compassion jumping straight off the page and into your heart.

You will also find questions and exercises to help you unlock your story and activate your healing. As Laura explains, we all have a story that has shaped and molded who we are. If we're courageous and lucky enough, our story eventually becomes our mission. Laura's story has become her great life's work, and we are all better because of it.

One of the lines in this book that shook me to my core was this: "We love and we suffer, and sharing the vulnerabilities of love and suffering is what builds our compassion."

We aren't meant to walk through this world alone. Life is filled with heartache and hope, and our ability to share the range of our human experience is what makes it so beautiful.

The Compassion Code is indeed a doorway into a beautiful life. May you be nourished by this book in the same ways I have been.

Julie Santiago
author, speaker, and transformational women's coach
www.juliesantiago.com

Introduction

After graduating from university, a few of my friends and I moved to Panama to pursue a dream. We decided to open a backpacker's hostel on an island in the Caribbean called Bocas del Toro. I was living in what we often called "Neverland," having the time of my life, meeting people from all over the world, and the icing on the cake was that I had just met the man I would later marry.

At what felt like a peak of joy, excitement, and fulfillment, I received the worst news of my life. I found out that my mom, my best friend, was killed in a tragic accident. She was doing something she did nearly every day: taking a walk. On this fateful day, she was crossing the street at the crosswalk, and the truck in her lane did not see her when the light turned green. He hit her and ran her over, and she was killed instantly.

While I didn't receive word for hours after the accident, that day became the most devastating and life-altering day of my life.

These are stories you hear about—they aren't your life. I immediately started making travel plans, figuring out logistics, and worrying about everyone else. As I look back, it is clear to see that I was in shock and that the best I could do was survive. I stayed in this practical, non-emotional, survival mode for nearly the entire first year.

My life as I had known it was over, and while I didn't know it at the time, a new chapter was just beginning. I knew I was still in there somewhere, but the light that had always shined so brightly in me had become so dim that I barely recognized myself.

While much of me felt defeated and hopeless, there was a tiny ember of hope that I would find myself again.

And I have.

I may not be the same carefree girl I once was, but I am instead a woman full of light, love, and compassion. I am a woman with purpose, who, while still on my healing journey, has the light back in her eyes.

I am not going to say that my journey has been easy, but I can tell you I have learned a tremendous amount along the way.

While we often try to hide our scars, these experiences are part of us, part of our story.

As I mentioned, people have always told me their stories, and I have always loved hearing them. Without recognizing it as a gift, I was always able to relate to people in a loving, nonjudgmental way.

However, I am also human, with my own idiosyncrasies and my own beliefs about the world. When my mom died, my world crumbled and the way I had always approached life no longer worked. The silver linings I had always found to help me through difficult times didn't feel helpful, and my ability to see the bright side began impeding my healing.

We often learn as much from what doesn't work as from what does. After working through the pain of my mom's death and then working for years with people who also experienced grief and loss, I have learned valuable lessons about the human heart, people's uniqueness, and how to help people heal.

My training as a Certified Grief Recovery Specialist and my experience training professionals for the Grief Recovery Institute have given me unique insight into the human experience of loss. The people I support through grief recovery continuously teach me what works and what doesn't when it comes to healing. The Grief Recovery Institute, as you will notice throughout the book, has taught me a great deal about how to support people as they traverse through their grief. If you haven't already, I urge you to read the Grief Recovery Handbook. It has given me tremendous insight and understanding about grief, and I am forever grateful. You will find some of its teachings in this book as well.

Compassion and understanding are why I am here. Something I know deeply is that everyone has a story and that each story is important. Curiosity about other people's stories is the groundwork of compassion. Exploring and reflecting upon our own stories is what helps us move toward self-compassion.

The thing is, life is hard sometimes: that's a fact. But having someone to talk to, to cry with, to sit with—even in silence—is a healing gift.

I am writing this book for you, offering my best tools and resources to help you be even more compassionate with your friends, family, partner, coworkers, clients, patients, and even yourself when it comes to loss, grief, and other challenges that arise through the course of our turbulent lives.

Today, you can figure almost anything out by searching Google or YouTube. You want to learn how to fish, how to tie a knot, how to study for a test, how to de-stress, how to ask a girl out, or pretty much anything else? Just Google it.

But when it comes to knowing what to say and do when you come across people who are struggling, very few people seem to know how to confidently communicate in a compassionate way.

I want to start by offering you two of my most basic tools to begin confidently communicating with compassion.

- First is your Compassion Hat. The Compassion Hat is key because it allows you to "step out of yourself" and practice non-judgment. When you put on your Compassion Hat, you can begin to imagine what someone else's story may be, aiding you in walking the proverbial mile in their shoes.

- Second is your Grief-Colored Glasses. You may be wondering what Grief-Colored Glasses have to do with compassion. These glasses are incredibly useful for understanding what influences people to act the way they do. The avoided, unresolved grief of the past is often what keeps people from being the best version of themselves.

As a Certified Grief Recovery Specialist, I have learned that grief is not just how we feel when someone dies. The definition used at the Grief Recovery Institute is "the conflicting feelings caused by the end of or change in a familiar pattern of behavior." This definition opens the grief experience to much more than death alone.

Death can certainly be a grieving experience, and yet there are many other losses we can experience in life. When things change, we experience grief. We feel relief and we feel sadness. We feel fear and excitement. We feel emptiness and freedom.

Our Grief-Colored Glasses allow us to see beyond the façade of "I'm fine," and let us see what people aren't telling us—the pain and unresolved grief that is not only normal but ever-present in every human being. Whether you have experienced the death of someone you love, had your heart broken, lost your dream job, had to put your childhood dog to sleep, or been diagnosed with cancer, we all walk around with our tales of grief.

By understanding that grief is everywhere because loss is part of the human experience, we can begin to grow our compassion muscle for both others and ourselves.

Now, with your Compassion Hat and Grief-Colored Glasses, you can begin journeying through life with a secret advantage. From here, the tools and resources you'll learn will be much easier to digest and put into practice. And, by utilizing these new tools, you will begin to connect with others in a way that promotes love, compassion, acceptance, unity, and understanding.

If your profession or personality require you to routinely exercise compassion, you may at times feel drained or saddened by the pain you're helping others process. For you, I will also be sharing tools that will allow your compassion to shine without burnout.

I write to you with deep love in my heart and hope you find greater compassion and confidence when communicating with people experiencing emotional pain. This book is just the beginning, and it feels so great to share it with you. Thank you for picking it up. It is meant for you.

PART I: THE COMPASSION BASICS

Chapter 1: What Compassion Is and Isn't

I wasn't born knowing what to say or do when people are suffering. On New Year's Eve of my senior year in college, I received the news that a good friend of mine from high school had lost her mom. I was stunned and my reaction was, looking back, a bit surprising.

I did nothing. I didn't call. I didn't go to the funeral. I didn't write.

You may be thinking that I was a terrible friend. How did I live with myself? Well, I justified it. I thought to myself, *I haven't talked to her in several years. She doesn't want to hear from me. I don't want to bother her. I don't know what I would say.*

At that point in my life, I considered myself a compassionate person. I deeply cared for people and loved my friend, but my response was anything but compassionate. Why?

I was scared. I simply didn't know what to do or say, and I was deeply afraid to say the wrong thing.

While I had been through a few loss experiences myself, I had always been able to find a reason that it had worked out for the best, a silver lining. But I couldn't think of a silver lining this time, so I merely resorted to radio silence.

What I know now, and why I tell you this story, is that it was not about being compassionate or not, it was about not having the tools, understanding, or experience to best support my friend. For years, I was incredibly hard on myself for how I responded in that situation. Now, I have compassion for myself that I simply didn't know, and now I get to do better.

Compassion is something you can develop and improve. The fact that you picked up this book shows me that you're a compassionate person (even if you haven't always had the most compassionate responses). With the tools and resources you'll learn in the following pages, you will be equipped with the ability to think, feel, act, and be compassionate.

As you start this journey, please join me with an open mind because there is a good chance that, if you are reading this book, you already have a lot of experience and education. I encourage you to take it one step further and engage this material with a beginner's mind. In other words, please read this book with curiosity rather than judgment, and look for the nuggets that resonate most with you. If you have heard some of this material before, get curious about how it affects you differently this time, because you are likely hearing it again for a reason. Or maybe it's time to put this knowledge into action, and perhaps reading this book can help give you the little nudge you need.

Together, we are going to create a world with more love, more understanding, and more compassion. When we see beyond the surface and get to know people for their stories, for their unique experiences, and for their distinct gifts, hate becomes impossible and love becomes inevitable.

We love and we suffer, and sharing the vulnerabilities of love and suffering is what builds our compassion.

I first learned this concept as a young girl. My family was highly involved with a foreign exchange program called AFS, the American Field Service. It began during World War I, when volunteer ambulance drivers were cruising around the battlefields and picking up the wounded soldiers, no matter which side they were on. Today, it's an international high school foreign exchange program that allows students from all around the world to go and live with a family in another nation for a year, a semester, or a summer.

The goal of AFS is to introduce young people to other people and their stories so they can return to their home with more maturity, understanding, love, and compassion for strangers, because those strangers, when you get to know them, are no longer strange. Students—like my father, brother, husband, and me—discovered that foreigners are people with stories, with children, with education, with community, with passion, with hobbies, with faith, and with love. And as I say to my daughter, "Strangers are just friends we haven't met yet."

When young people experience other cultures, their perspective of the world deepens. They no longer need to judge based on clothing, language, religion, or politics; rather, they get to know the stories of the people who live in that new place. It is about embracing their similarities and appreciating their differences.

By hosting students throughout early years and then going abroad myself, this concept became ingrained in me. It has become a foundational value of my life.

As someone who has had the unique opportunity to travel all around the world, live in other countries, and host visitors in the United States, I have dedicated myself to being an ambassador of goodwill. However, it wasn't always this way. In 2003, one month after the Iraq War began, I moved down to Santiago, Chile. The people I met were well informed and often knew more about what was going on in my country than I did. At that point, it was hard to be from the United States (much less Texas) because we weren't loved on the world stage, and I wasn't sure what my beliefs were.

To avoid conflict or heated conversation, I began telling people I was Canadian. However, the more I traveled, the more I realized I was doing myself, my country, and the world a disservice. So instead of lying about my origins, I began stepping into my role as an ambassador of goodwill.

I knew that telling the truth about myself as a loving, compassionate, open-minded, curious person would be more impactful. By making deep connections with people throughout the world, as myself, there was a chance that one day that person would go back to their home country and say, "I met this nice Texas girl once. . . ." And perhaps they would think, *You know Americans aren't so bad. I met one I liked in my travels.*

As a managing partner of several hostels in Panama, this was my underlying mission—to plant seeds of friendship, love, and understanding that would one day blossom to make the world a more connected, compassionate place.

Relating Kindly to Ourselves

A friend recently went through a breakup from a long-term relationship. After receiving pressure from family and friends to "get back out there," she finally gave in. She went on a blind date and it seemed to be going well. But about half an hour into the date, he walked out on her without an explanation. She called her friend in tears and her friend said, "Of course he walked out. You're overweight, unattractive, and have a ton of baggage."

If you are gasping at the mean-natured response of her supposed friend, you're not alone.

Now, what if I told you those weren't her friends' words, but rather the things she told herself? While still awful, it might seem less appalling because self-criticism is something most people experience.[1]

That being said, the first step to love and compassion is to relate kindly to ourselves. When we start there, even if it is just baby steps, we will be able to be more loving and compassionate toward others.

Compassion is about finding the balance between sympathy— feeling *for* someone, and empathy—feeling *with* someone. It is, as neuroscientist Max Planck says, "experiencing feelings of loving-kindness toward another person's affliction."[2]

On the bell curve of compassion, both extremes can lead to disconnection. It looks like:

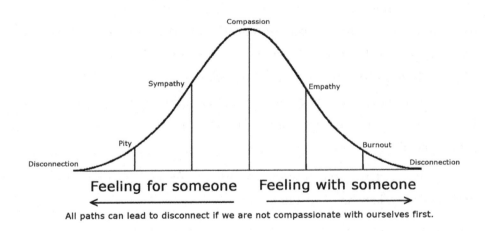

All paths can lead to disconnect if we are not compassionate with ourselves first.

Though related, compassion need not be mistaken for empathy. Compassion is about loving-kindness for other people's suffering, while "empathy refers to the ability to relate to another person's pain

---

1   Adaptation from Guy Winch: Why we all need to practice emotional first aid – TED.com

2   https://www.ncbi.nlm.nih.gov/pubmed/22661409

vicariously, as if one has experienced that pain themselves."[3] Empathy can lead to burnout and disconnection because it can be overwhelming to consistently feel other people's pain.

Compassion allows you to connect without falling into the depths of despair, which allows for a more supportive connection. When I teach the Grief Recovery Certification Training, I share that if you tear up when someone is sharing their story with you, it can be a beautiful form of compassion. However, if someone's story has you cocooned on the floor sobbing, you can no longer support them.

No matter where you are in life, relationships are the glue of families, effective and profitable working environments, governance, and local and global economy. Therefore, when we're compassionate, we can see other people's perspectives, which allows us to understand each other more easily, and thus create more peace and safety. We can love more deeply and experience more joy. We can experience more vulnerability, and consequently, more connection. We can build community, which in turn creates more belonging. And with all of this, we create more personal satisfaction and more hope for a future that serves us all.

We also get to have fewer misunderstandings, fewer fights, less fear, less hurt, less hate, and less war.

I don't know about you, but I believe that compassion for self and others may very well be the answer to healing our hurt, hate-filled world.

Unfortunately, becoming more compassionate isn't always simple. What gets in the way of us being more compassionate and loving toward the people we know and the strangers we come across?

Perhaps it's our lack of understanding of their affliction. Perhaps

---

3   https://www.merriam-webster.com/dictionary/empathy

it's our lack of desire to understand. Perhaps it's our fear of feeling too much. Perhaps it's when we are in the depth of our own pain that we lack compassion for others. When we hurt, when we feel sad, when we feel bad physically, mentally, or emotionally, it can be exhausting to be loving and compassionate toward others.

Here is a beautiful testament of Todd Nigro, founder of Ellie's Way, who learned about compassion for self and others through the devastating experience of losing his six-year-old daughter.

Before Ellie died, I took my son to his baseball hitting lesson. We really liked the instructor, and being friendly I asked him, "How many kids do you have?" He informed me that he had two sons, but one had committed suicide several years before. I remember being shocked and at a complete loss as to what to do or say. I think I probably looked very uncomfortable, and I was. I don't remember exactly what happened, but I probably changed the subject, and I would bet that I didn't offer up very much in the way of comfort.

Before Ellie died, I was afraid of death, pain, and suffering. I didn't want to experience any of those things for myself, and it was scary to see in other people. I didn't know what to say, how to feel, what to do, so the easiest thing was to avoid thinking about it. Sadly, I had never been to a funeral before Ellie's.

Before Ellie died, I didn't appreciate taking her to the costume jewelry store or playing with her dolls. I enjoyed our bedtime routine of reading and snuggling, but I always wanted to leave before she wanted me to. I had things to do. Later I asked myself, "What was so important?"

Well, things change. After losing six-year-old Ellie, I have learned a few things.

I give people the benefit of the doubt, and I assume that they care, even if it doesn't seem like it. The fact is that unless you've experienced a deep loss, it is hard to empathize and understand. I try to help people with their reactions and make it easy for them if I can. I know that I needed some help and guidance over the prior years.

When I saw the baseball instructor at a game a few months ago, I jumped up and walked over to him. I told him about the conversation we had many years ago, and I apologized for my insensitivity and lack of understanding. Although the circumstances of our children's deaths were different, we were both fathers without our babies. We shared a hug and a few tears, and it was a memorable moment.

Now I always go to the funeral, for whomever has passed away. I have been to many in the past five years, and I've volunteered to help as needed. It is crucial to support the grieving families by simply being there for them.

One day, leaving the grocery store, I walked past a group of little girls, a dad, and a table full of Girl Scout cookies. I was late and did not intend to purchase anything, but the father said, "How about some cookies?" I said, "No, thank you," to which he replied, "You must not have a little girl at home. You're lucky!" The tears quickly flowed as I continued walking. It was a difficult moment, but I soon realized that could have been me with Ellie, a father who wasn't exactly excited about selling Girl Scout cookies. We are all on a journey and life has a way of teaching us.

I take the time to be with my family and friends, and to savor the moments. I am thankful for each day with my loved ones and try to bring a smile and some joy to the world. I've learned that kindness, compassion, and service to others brings deep meaning and purpose. Loving people through all of the circumstances of life is a good plan.

I was recently at a golf lesson with my son, and his instructor was talking to me. Then he asked the inevitable question in a friendly way: "How many kids do you have?"

And so it goes . . .

Returning to the woman whose blind date walked out on her, how could she show compassion toward herself and her date?

First, by relating kindly toward herself and acknowledging that the hurt she felt was natural. Second, by considering that he may have left for a completely different reason than what she thought, and likely it had nothing to do with her being inadequate.

If she was being kind to herself, she may think, *I wonder what happened,* rather than, *What's wrong with me.*

Admittedly, I haven't always loved myself. As a teenage girl, I didn't like my body. Puberty was both physically and emotionally painful, as growing can be. My body and my hormones were changing, and I felt like it was all out of my control. I was grieving my more carefree days of childhood while entering into being a woman with a lot of uncertainty.

The societal pressure to be "beautiful" and fit a certain image was overwhelming, and my female role models subscribed to the same standards of self-criticism, dieting, and body shame. I honestly didn't know there was any other way.

When I was pregnant with my daughter, I decided that I no longer wanted to give credence to the negative self-talk and body hate I had allowed to infiltrate my thoughts throughout my teens and twenties. I wanted to lead by example for my daughter, and that meant loving myself and my body. The thought of her hating herself was enough motivation to enroll in a program called Body Love with my dear friend and colleague, Richele Henry.

After spending several months creating awareness around body love, I realized that it is a learned skill that takes practice, just like compassion. This was a relief because it meant that I could continue improving.

According to the "conscious competence" learning model, there is a process of progressing from incompetence to competence in any skill. It suggests that:

Individuals are initially unaware of how little they know, or unconscious of their incompetence. As they recognize their incompetence, they consciously acquire a skill, then consciously use it. Eventually, the skill can be utilized without it being consciously thought through: the individual is said to have then acquired unconscious competence."[4]

While most of us start with unconscious incompetence, by simply realizing you lack body love, self-compassion, or any skill for that matter, you have already moved to conscious incompetence.

It all begins, therefore, with awareness that you don't know something. In that awareness, self-compassion is ready to bloom.

Compassion In Action: Relating kindly toward others starts with relating kindly toward yourself. I invite you to take a baby step toward self-compassion. Next time you look in the mirror, give yourself a little smile and say some version of, "You are okay." If you feel like stepping it up a notch, give yourself a compliment. Try doing this at least once a day.

---

4   Flower, J. "In the Mush." *Physician Executive.* 25 (1) (2009): 64–6.

Compassion Is NOT About Condoning Behavior

Often people don't want to allow themselves to feel compassion because they think it somehow means we are letting people get away with "unacceptable behavior." One important thing to remember when putting on your Compassion Hat is that feeling compassion for someone else DOES NOT mean you are condoning their behavior or admitting that you have done something wrong.

Understanding the Story Doesn't Justify the Behavior

It can be as simple as this: finding compassion for people who cause us pain or who do "terrible" things is partially for our own sanity. This type of compassion can provide us with more peace in our lives by crowding out negative thought patterns. My anger and pain does not make what someone else did go away; it merely hurts me and adds to the negative energy.

Here is an example.

On one of my work trips, I met a woman who had had a fight with her adult son.

As I walked into the lobby to check in, I noticed her in the corner crying on the phone. I could not hear what she was saying, but she was visibly distraught. About an hour later, while I was eating dinner in the hotel restaurant, she approached me and within a couple of minutes, she was sharing the circumstances that led her to this moment.

In short, she was visiting her son, and they had had a miscommunication that led to an altercation. He asked her to leave in a wounding way, and she proceeded to the hotel after the hurtful exchange.

I listened to her experience and acknowledged the pain she was feeling. We talked about what may have caused him to act that way and recognized that his words and actions were likely not about her, but rather a buildup and projection of how he was feeling about himself. I encouraged her to take care of herself, as the only thing she could control was her own response to the situation.

The next day before she left, she asked me what to do. She said, "I don't want to leave here without communicating with him, but I also don't want him to think what he did is okay." Meaning, she wanted to show compassion without condoning his behavior.

Together, we composed a text that said something like:

Son, I'm leaving today. Seeing that life is short and we don't know what tomorrow will bring, I didn't want to leave without saying I love you. I'm sad and disappointed with the way things were left between us, and I hope we can reconcile at some point. Until then, I'm going to go home and take care of myself, and I hope you can do the same.
Mom

Being compassionate does not mean that we trivialize our feelings or experience, nor does it mean ignoring justice. It is about finding a balance between acknowledging the hurt without carrying resentment, and considering the other person's experience without justifying their behavior.

Compassion Is Freedom

Being compassionate toward others also involves forgiveness, of both self and others. However, as I teach it in Grief Recovery, the challenge with forgiveness is that we, as a society, have made it synonymous with condoning. The difference according to Merriam-Webster is this:

- Forgive: to cease to feel resentment against (an offender)
- Condone: to regard or treat (something bad or blameworthy) as acceptable, forgivable, or harmless

As you can see, these two concepts are not the same.

Compassionate Coaching Tip: Forgiveness is actually for you, not for the other. Forgiveness is about letting go of resentment so that you can be free of any hurt you are carrying.

"Resentment is the poison we take in hopes that someone else dies" is a quote attributed to various people—Nelson Mandela, Malachy McCourt, and Carrie Fisher. While the exact origin is unclear, what is clear is when we refuse to put on our Compassion Hat and instead hold onto resentment, we hold onto our own pain, potentially becoming what we resent or don't understand.

People typically don't want to be around angry, violent people. This mindset can lead to isolation and loneliness, which reduce our happiness, health, and longevity according to *The Lonely American* by psychiatrists Jacqueline Olds and Richard Schwartz.

While feeling the feelings is important—be it frustration, sadness, or anger—if you let any one emotion become who you are, you will likely find yourself disconnected from others, your community, and your most authentic self.

This story about the Amish community really impacted me and is a beautiful example of compassion and forgiveness.

Following the tragic shooting in October 2006 of ten young girls in a one-room Amish school, reporters from throughout the world invaded Lancaster County, PA, to cover the story. However, in the hours and days following the shooting, a different, unexpected story developed.

In the midst of their grief during this shocking loss, the Amish community didn't cast blame, point fingers, or hold a press conference with attorneys at their sides. Instead, they reached out with grace and compassion toward the killer's family.

The afternoon of the shooting, an Amish grandfather of one of the girls who was killed expressed forgiveness toward the shooter, Charles Roberts. That same day, Amish neighbors visited the Roberts family to comfort them in their sorrow and pain.

Later that week, the Roberts family was invited to the funeral of one of the Amish girls. In a compassionate twist, Amish mourners outnumbered the non-Amish at Charles Roberts' funeral.

What came to light was that the killer was tormented for nine years by the premature death of his young daughter, and he never forgave God for her death. Yet, after he cold-bloodedly shot ten innocent schoolgirls, the Amish almost immediately forgave him and showed compassion toward his family.

In a world at war and in a society that often points fingers and blames others, this reaction was unheard of. Many reporters and interested followers of the story asked, "How could they forgive such a terrible, unprovoked act of violence against innocent lives?"

The Amish culture closely follows the teachings of Jesus, who taught his followers to forgive one another, to place the needs of others before themselves, and to rest in the knowledge that God is still in control and can bring good out of any situation. Love and compassion toward others is meant to be our life's theme. Vengeance and revenge is to be left to God.[5]

We don't always get to choose.

We don't choose our family, where we are born, the color of our skin, our body type, the faith or belief system that our families have, or our children. We often don't get to choose what happens to us either.

However, we do get to choose how we respond and how we live our lives. So, with the few choices we have, let's be intentional and choose compassion.

 **Compassion in Action:** If you could let go of resentment against someone in your life, who would it be? If they were to apologize to you, what would you want them to say? Write yourself a short note from them with the apology and be sure to include what you think they may be going through. Read the letter to yourself aloud or allow a safe friend to read it to you.[6]

---

5   http://lancasterpa.com/amish/amish-forgiveness/

6   This is an adaptation of an exercise I learned from Dr. Shawne Duperon of Project Forgive. http://projectforgive.com/

Compassion Is Living with Intention

Choosing compassion is one of the few choices we do have that can improve our lives and make the world better. By putting on our Compassion Hat and recognizing that everyone has a story, we can choose love and learn to let go of resentment.

Much of my compassion for others was born from growing up as a Jewish girl in Texas. I was different, and as a young person, that isn't fun or easy. In the Bible Belt of the United States with a church on every corner, it definitely didn't seem okay that I was Jewish. The thing I often felt frustrated by was the fact that I didn't choose my religion; I was merely born into a Jewish family who happened to live in Sugar Land, Texas. Oddly enough, even though Sugar Land is quite culturally diverse, because I am white, most people were confused as to why I wasn't Christian.

I found myself either hiding the fact that I was Jewish or defending my Jewish heritage. In high school, I was told by several friends that they wished they could save me from hell. At fifteen, this was devastating because I didn't know what I had done wrong. By the time I went to college, I had grown shameful of being Jewish because it was an intrinsic part of me for which I was being judged. It wasn't until I went to college, where I met many other Jews who shared both my religion and worldview, that I began to accept this part of myself.

As I have transitioned into adulthood, traveled the world, and learned to accept myself, I've grown to appreciate this difference and anything that makes me unique.

After experiencing discrimination for something I didn't choose, I decided that I would do my best to accept others as they are. Knowing the pain of judgment led me down a clear path of compassion and love.

In recent years, I have realized that compassion and acceptance build connection. Accepting people as they are isn't always easy, but since I don't like being judged, I don't want to judge. It's probably the reason why people on the plane, in the market, at a dinner party, or anywhere else are inclined to share their life stories with me. Perhaps it is partially because I listen without judgment and partially because it is clear that I genuinely care.

So, being a Jewish girl in Texas was a gift, because it helped me accept people of all faiths, cultures, colors, sizes, and sexual orientations—because, as Lady Gaga put it best, "Baby, we were born this way." We are hard enough on ourselves. What if we could show ourselves and others a little compassion?

How can we judge someone for the color of their skin or who they want to be intimate with when we have never lived in their body, heart, or mind?

Our differences are what make life interesting if we allow them to. As one of my mentors, Stacey Morgenstern, said, "Curiosity is the cure for judgment."

Compassionate Coaching Tip: We have so much to learn from one another, but we have to begin approaching each other with curiosity rather than judgment. When we do, it becomes safer for people to share the best version of themselves with us.

Compassion In Action Part I: Expanding your compassion can come from talking to people who aren't like you. Try having a meaningful conversation with a stranger this week and be curious about who they are.

Compassion In Action Part II: Is there a part of your identity that you have rejected because of shame? What is it and what is one step you could take towards integrating that part of yourself back into your complete identity? (Hint: find a small group or community of people who share in this aspect of your identity.)

A Note on Judgment Versus Being Nonjudgmental

I am not suggesting we vilify judgment, as it is a natural and important part of human nature. As defined by Merriam-Webster, judgment is "the ability for reaching a decision after careful consideration." Careful discernment helps keep us safe and allows us to make decisions. When I am suggesting we not judge others or ourselves, I am talking about being nonjudgmental, which is, "not judged or judging on the basis of one's personal standards or opinions.[7]"

See the difference? Making a judgment is about making a decision based upon careful consideration. Being nonjudgmental is about not letting personal bias impact action or interaction.

---

7   http://www.dictionary.com/

Chapter 2: When is Compassion Really Needed?

When we think about situations where we'd be inclined to be compassionate, it's easy to imagine with someone who is dealing with circumstances outside their control, like death or job loss. But it's not always easy to find compassion when approaching someone whose path doesn't make sense to us, such as addictive, uncivil, or unethical behavior.

For example, when we come across someone using drugs in an alley, we may say to ourselves, "That's so pathetic," or "What a weak person." But what if we asked ourselves, "What may have happened in their life that led them here?" The truth is, this behavior may, in fact, not feel like a choice for that person, but rather a coping tool.

The following situations are opportunities to put on our Compassion Hat, even when it feels like a stretch. Again, I want to emphasize that we make these choices not only for our own freedom, but also to be an example of the light we wish to see in the world.

Different Kinds of Compassion

Compassion for self: *Relating kindly to self. Giving permission to feel.*

Why: As human beings we are imperfect, and compassion for self is understanding and accepting that. We all deserve love, and we can only receive as much love from others as we give to ourselves. The more we nourish ourselves with compassion, the more ability we will have to share it with others.

Compassion for strangers: *Recognizing that everyone has a story that explains why they are who they are and do what they do.*

Why: When we have compassion for strangers and we give them the benefit of the doubt, we are more likely to create connections, have kinder interactions, and build a world with more love and acceptance. More love and acceptance leads to less hatred, less isolation, and fewer incidents of violence.

Compassion for family and friends: *Relating kindly to the people we know. Realizing that even though we know them, we can't always read their minds or understand their map of the world. The more we incorrectly assume we know, the more likely our judgment will get in the way of our curiosity.*

Why: We can have healthier relationships and less resentment when we step back and take a curious look at the story, rather than a judgmental one. When we don't assume we know what someone is experiencing, they are more likely to share their truth.

Compassion for people who anger you (strangers or family): *Judging others reveals an unhealed part of yourself.*

Why: You may not like this, but this is a chance to look in the mirror. It is an opportunity for growth. Finding compassion when people upset you allows you to create more peace in your daily life by not spending so much energy focused outward on what's wrong with someone else. Rather, you can focus inward on why this situation or person's behavior is bothering you.

Compassion for people in an emotional emergency: *Being gentle and understanding with people when they are in crisis (whether YOU think it is a crisis or not).*

Why: If we can be compassionate, slow to judge, and not take things personally, we can allow others to have their experience and not be so affected by it. When people are in an emotional emergency, they may not act the way they normally would, and the best thing to do is remind ourselves, "This is not about me."

Compassion for people who are grieving: *When people experience loss of any kind, they often lose a sense of who they are. Compassion for a griever means allowing them to feel and to have their own experience without thinking it "should" be a certain way.*

Why: Grief is everywhere. Life can be painful and difficult, and relating kindly to people in their grief experience creates a safe environment and a deeper connection. When grievers feel compassion directed their way, they don't have to isolate themselves or hide their feelings, which can prevent misdirected explosive behaviors from road rage to abuse.

Compassion for a killer or someone who does something horrible: *Knowing that deeply hurt people are often the ones who hurt other people.*

Why: If you carry resentment and hatred, it's only hurting you, and hatred begets hatred.

Compassion for patients or clients: *Knowing that there is a unique story behind every person you work with and that they have come into your office for your growth as well.*

Why: Whether it is your job to know your patients/clients or not, the connection you create with them, and your understanding of their world, is what makes you successful, fulfilled, and effective without burnout.

Compassion for a group: *Relating kindly to groups of people who have different life experiences and who do things differently from you.*

Why: When we look at a group of people we don't understand (because they may eat different foods, speak different languages, wear different clothes, learn differently, live in different environments, worship differently, etc.) and find the value in our differences, we get to create more love and acceptance in the world and broaden our own horizons. As John Steinbeck wrote: "It means very little to know that a million Chinese are starving unless you know one Chinese who is starving."

PART II: LAYING THE FOUNDATION

Chapter 3: Compassion Takes Practice

"We but mirror the world. All the tendencies present in the outer world are to be found in the world of our body. If we could change ourselves, the tendencies in the world would also change. As a man changes his own nature, so does the attitude of the world change towards him. This is the divine mystery supreme. A wonderful thing it is and the source of our happiness. We need not wait to see what others do." —Mahatma Gandhi

Many people share that they feel inadequate when it comes to responding in challenging situations. They either fumble with their words, say nothing, or say the completely wrong thing. Thinking, speaking, acting, and even being compassionate are not things that happen easily or immediately. To reiterate, compassion is something you must practice continuously if you want it to make a difference in your daily life, improve your interactions, and make the world a better place.

When you find yourself frustrated, angry, upset, or simply lacking understanding, remind yourself to put on your Compassion Hat. We aren't perfect; we are human. Compassion takes practice.

Here are a few more things you can focus on as you practice compassion:

Let go of a judgmental mindset. Judgment obviously has its place—it is useful when we are analyzing risk, choosing a partner, or making other hard decisions. However, judgment doesn't have much of a place with compassion because it gets in the way of love. When we are judging, we think we know better or are better than someone else. For the purposes of compassion and connection, judgment is a no-go. Remember the idea that when you compare, you despair? By saying that mine is more important than yours, we are alienating and diminishing, which is the opposite of compassion.

Let go of assuming that you know. In order to be compassionate, you have to know that you don't always know. We don't know what people are going through, and we therefore have to let go of thinking we do. We judge from our map of the world, but it is important to remind ourselves that everyone sees the world with a different lens. When we let go of thinking we know, we can make room for listening with curiosity. Curiosity is a principal ingredient for compassion.

Let go of thinking it's about you. It is almost never about you. People are typically thinking and judging themselves. When someone acts out with anger or rudeness, take a deep breath and say to yourself, "This is not about me." Most likely they have a story underneath with some unresolved pain. While it isn't fair for them to take it out on you, you can diffuse the situation by not taking it personally.

Compassionate Coaching Tip: If it feels personal, a great question to ask yourself is, "What can I learn from this experience?" Someone once said, everything you hear or experience, even eavesdropping, is there for your growth.

Let go of your need to fix the situation. Another tip I learned from the Grief Recovery Institute is that just because someone is suffering from a broken heart doesn't mean they are broken. When we think we have to fix someone, we lose sight of our mission to be compassionate. It is hard to *do* and *be* at the same time. If we are to *be* compassionate, then we have to let go of fixing. Advice-giving falls under fixing, and unless someone asks for advice, there's no need to give it. We want so badly to make it all better, but ultimately, the person is having his or her experience. Our only job is to be compassionate.

Surprisingly, you don't have to say much to be compassionate, as there is rarely a response that will make it better. It's really about being there for others with love and presence, without judgment or comparison.

By viewing compassion as a practice, we can take the pressure off ourselves to be perfect in our communication. When we catch ourselves judging, fixing, or advice-giving without permission, rather than beating ourselves up, we can take the opportunity to practice self-compassion. When we relate kindly to ourselves by first acknowledging that we, ourselves, are human, it is much easier to find our way back to compassion.

Compassion In Action: Practice some of your new tools. Next time someone shares what they are going through, pause, take a breath, reserve your inclination to offer a solution, and acknowledge and validate what they are experiencing.

Chapter 4: Whose Map Are You Standing On?

One of the theories I learned during my training to become a health coach at the Institute of Integrative Nutrition is the idea of bio-individuality. In short, "No perfect way of eating works for everybody. The food that works for your unique body, age, and lifestyle may make another person gain weight and feel lethargic. Similarly, no perfect way of eating will work for you all the time."[8]

The reason I bring up this concept is because bio-individuality isn't only for food. It is also true for how we experience life, how we move through our pain, how we grow, how resilient we are, and just about every other aspect of life. For now, we are focused on being compassionate toward ourselves and others, and recognizing that we grieve differently. While suffering is a human experience and universal feelings do exist, we must also remember that everyone's map of the world is unique.

When I talk about a map of the world, it isn't merely about a physical point of view. It is about the experiences we bring to the table up until this point. It is about the beliefs that we have formed throughout our lives. Our individual belief system is how we experience the world.

The fascinating thing is that we all have a different map. When it

---

8   Rosenthal, Joshua. *Integrative Nutrition*. Integrative Nutrition Publishing, 2014. pg 35.

comes to compassion, we can recognize that our viewpoint is different than the next person's, even if that person is someone we are close to like a parent, a sibling, a friend, or a spouse.

When I lead Grief Recovery Certification trainings, I do an exercise where I ask each participant to tell me the first thought that comes to mind when I say a few different words. This is also referred to by psychologists as word association. I would like you to try it now (Remember, there is no wrong answer).

- Dog
- Water
- Knife
- Money

What came to mind for you?

The typical response for the word dog generally ranges from love, to slobber, to cat, to Fluffy, to fear, and there are always others in between. The person who says love or who says their dog's name is often surprised that someone else's word is fear. What about water? The typical response for this one usually ranges from play, to ocean, to relaxing, to hydration, to drowning. Again, those who thought of peaceful and beautiful images were taken aback by the fact that someone else's first response was drowning. Knife and money are the same. The responses range from sushi to murder and from freedom to greed.

Whatever your response, it can help you understand your perspective a little bit more. These unique responses and thoughts illustrate our bio-individuality. Each of us has a unique map built from our own experiences and misunderstandings that often come from the fact that we don't understand someone else's map.

Part of building compassion is understanding that we are all unique. We grieve differently. We heal differently. Some of us wear black all the time, while others love wearing bright colors. We speak different languages and had different experiences in school, the rules our parents taught us, and so on. When we can accept the beauty in our differences and accept ourselves and others, our relationships and the world around us can begin to heal. Accepting others' experiences is part of being compassionate.

My brother and I both lost our mom to the same tragedy, and we both suffered deep pain. However, because of our bio-individuality, our unique relationships with our mom, and our individual personalities, we grieved her death very differently.

My brother was much more expressive with his feelings. He started a project where he interviewed everyone who ever knew our mom. Because of his love for writing, interviewing people, and connecting, it was the perfect way for him to grieve her death and honor her life. After talking to hundreds of people from our mom's life, he compiled the stories and made a book for our dad. It is an incredible gift, and it was a key part of his healing journey.

My process was quite different. I pretended I was "fine" for many months, but at some point the pain had to find its way out. I went to massage school, became a health coach, found life coaching, and eventually discovered the Grief Recovery Institute. In essence, my grief journey led me to my life's work.

Once we accepted each other's process, we were able to connect through our shared suffering, and our love for each other also deepened.

Unfortunately, it is common to have families torn apart because of their bio-individuality. A couple who loses a child may each grieve differently over the death. This disparity can cause tremendous pressure on a relationship, and without the understanding that we are all unique and different in our reactions, we can feel very alone. Couples often divorce after the death of their child because they become alienated from one another. One might think, *They don't care because they're not crying.*

The truth may be that one of the parents is trying to be strong for the other, rather than being vulnerable and saying, "I'm really struggling too."

When putting on your Compassion Hat, remember that each person experiences the world differently, and that is more than okay. Being aware that each person's process is distinct—not better or worse—can help us be compassionate.

Compassion In Action: We talk about walking a mile in another person's shoes. How can you bring this to life? Consider volunteering during your vacation, visit a different religious center, or attend a meeting that you would typically criticize. Remember, try this with curiosity not judgment.

Chapter 5: Everyone Has a Story (Including You)

We all were born, had parents or guardians, went to school, made friends, got teased, lost someone we loved (be it a pet, a friend who moved away, a grandparent, etc.), had some romantic interest that did or didn't materialize, went through a breakup, or weren't accepted to an internship, job, school, or group of friends that we wanted. You get the idea. That's life.

While each of us has distinct tales of trials and tribulations, joys and sorrows, love and hate, we all have one thing in common.

We all have a story.

If we lived in some future fantasy world where we had our story plastered across our foreheads, other people would have a better understanding of why we are the way we are. One of my tendencies is to give people the benefit of the doubt by considering what their story may be. And, if I get the chance, I ask because I enjoy learning about people's lives.

This characteristic allows me to connect with most people I meet because I am honestly interested in them. I approach others with a strong sense of compassion and curiosity, which allows them to open up—particularly on plane flights!

It began when I was quite young. One morning when my mom was driving me to school, someone cut her off and we were nearly in an accident. Naturally, she was upset because we could have been hurt. Her response came out of fear and love, but my immediate response was, "Mom, we're okay. Maybe that man is rushing to the hospital to see his wife."

I remember this moment clearly because she smiled and asked me, "What made you think that?"

I said, "You never know, Mom. Everyone has a story."

My mom was so touched by this that she quoted me for the rest of her life. During my teenage years, if I was ever being mistreated at school or feeling frustrated by a situation, she first acknowledged my hurt and then reminded me, "Laura, everyone has a story."

This line became my mantra in life. Most people aren't terrible, horrible, mean people; they are often in pain or have long been misunderstood.

It may seem idealistic to think this way, but what I can guarantee is that if you start to practice that way of thinking, you will begin seeing people in a whole new way—and likely with more compassion and understanding.

Compassionate Coaching Tip: Next time you react with anger or frustration, remember that everyone has a story. Think of something really hard that you never want to happen to you, and then imagine they are going through that. It is a great exercise at building compassion.

One of my past clients was complaining about how her mom and sister were being controlling and even rude about her upcoming wedding. I acknowledged how frustrating and upsetting that was for her, and then I offered her a different perspective.

If all acts are either a cry for love or an act of love[9], what does she think her mom and sister's behavior was?

She took a moment to consider this, then replied, "They're crying for love. They want to be involved, and I haven't let them." We talked about some ways she could let them participate in aspects of her wedding—those she maybe didn't care as much about—as a sign of love. Moving forward, she had a lot more compassion for them, and they were therefore much kinder to her.

Have you ever run into someone at the grocery store who was clearly having a terrible day? Perhaps they were ringing you up and you asked them how they were. They probably answered with some version of "I'm fine," yet they may have been lying, because fine rarely means fine.

Or perhaps they told the truth. "I'm okay," "Not so good," "Tired," "Great," "Ready to go home," "Sad." How did you respond? It is hard to know how to respond sometimes when people actually tell the truth, in part because we aren't used to it.

Compassion in Action: Practice asking people how they are and waiting for the answer. If they share a story or a feeling that is a little more vulnerable than "I'm fine," or "I'm great," you can practice saying some version of, "Thank you so much for sharing that with me." Depending on the situation you can add, "I hope you feel better or that your day improves," or "I'm sorry you have to go through that."

---

9   Paradigm of the Transformational Coaching Method [author or attribute?]

I share the idea that everyone has a story, not to give people an excuse to be a jerk, cranky, unfriendly, or cold, but so that you can choose to be compassionate and not let someone else's mood affect the rest of your day.

When we take people's attitude, rudeness, or anger personally, two people are now feeling upset instead of only one. Understanding (and remembering) that everyone has a story allows us to be more loving and compassionate, and it allows us to realize it is almost never about us.

A friend shared the following story with me, and I feel like it perfectly illustrates this point.

One night she went to a charity gala, the kind of event where you might buy a new dress or even wear a tuxedo. She had been preparing for over a month and when she arrived at the gala, she said it reminded her of a party from *The Great Gatsby*, with everyone beaming with anticipation.

She found her table and was thrilled to be sitting with the wife of the host of the event. When the master of ceremonies began, the emcee's wife stumbled in. She was seemingly intoxicated, her dress was not zipped all the way, and her hair looked like it hadn't been washed in days.

My friend was disappointed and disgusted, and she thought to herself, *How dare she be so disrespectful to show up this way.* When there was a break, she boldly approached the woman and said, "What's wrong with you?"

The woman responded with sadness in her eyes and said, "If you must know, just a few hours ago, I had to take my oldest child to a mental institution that he may never be able to leave. It was court ordered as he's considered a danger to my other children. I'm devastated. I haven't showered in days, but I have to be here because my husband's hosting the event."

In that moment, because of the woman's extreme honesty, my friend's life changed forever. She realized that this woman had a lot more going on than she could have ever imagined. She also decided that from that day forward, she would do her best to be compassionate toward people, because you never know what they are going through.

So remember, when you are aware or might have a hunch that another person isn't doing so great, ask them, with compassion and curiosity, "What's going on?" And be prepared to listen to the answer.

Realizing that they have a story will also free you from the handcuffs of thinking their behavior is somehow your fault. It is almost never about you. And when it is, there is almost always a lesson for your growth.

If you happen to be a person who actually wants to take the time to go deeper into someone's story, I will help you achieve this later. But for now, it all begins with awareness, curiosity, and compassion.

If everyone has a story, and you are someone, you have a story too.

* * * *

Understanding your own story can be an incredibly helpful way to approach the world with more compassion. Often, we are so wrapped up in the outer world that we forget to look inward and reflect on ourselves. Sometimes, we do this on purpose to avoid the pain of looking at our story. We are so afraid of uncovering the pain or admitting buried pain that we project our pain outward, many times at those we love.

Knowing and understanding your story can help you understand yourself, others, and the world you live in. You may be afraid to uncover a painful past, but I want you to know that having it buried away inside of you is more likely to harm you than if you were to let it out.

Do not, however, get stuck in your story. While everyone has a story, it doesn't have to define you, just as the past doesn't have to define you. Likewise, your parents' story doesn't have to be your story, because *you* are the narrator of your life, and you get to decide how your story is told.

After I graduated from college, there was a time when I was living in Panama, and my family didn't quite understand why I was living and working abroad. During one of my visits home, I overheard my dad telling some family friends that I was lost and trying to find my way. I was disappointed that he wasn't prouder of what I had accomplished; from my map of the world, I had taken a huge risk, moved to Central America with college friends, and been a major player in opening, operating, and improving two hostels and a bar on an island in the Caribbean (all utilizing my degree in Spanish).

Later that day, I was out for a walk with my friend and shared through my tears the sadness I felt that my dad wasn't proud of me. This friend's words stay with me to this day. He said, "Laura, you get to decide how you tell your story. Are you a lost hippie, or are you an international entrepreneur?"

I smiled through my tears, laughed, and said, "I'm an international entrepreneur who is bringing people from all over the world together in a safe, fun environment."

Compassion In Action: Relating kindly toward others starts with relating kindly toward yourself. I invite you to take a baby step toward self-compassion. Next time you look in the mirror, give yourself a little smile and say some version of, "You are okay." If you feel like stepping it up a notch, give yourself a compliment. Try doing this at least once a day.

Your story is key to unlocking your power, your communication, your connections, and your relationship with yourself, others, and the world.

William Bridges, who wrote *Making Sense of Life's Transitions*, encourages you to do an exercise that takes an inventory of all the losses and life transitions you have experienced.

Take some time to journal or reflect on the following questions:

What was your childhood like?

What did you want to be when you grew up?

How do you spend your days now?

What are some of the meaningful relationships of your life?

What are three accomplishments you are proud of?

What do you wish you could do more of?

What would you do differently if you could go back and change something about yourself?

What is a lesson you have learned from your children or other children in your life?

If today were your last day on Earth, how would you spend it?

If you answered all of these questions, then you are scratching the surface of your story. What did you learn about yourself? Note: See the back of the book for more questions to get to know yourself better.

When you understand your story, your joy, and your pain, you realize that the biggest lessons in life are learned from the greatest challenges we face.

It has been said that our challenges are our greatest gifts. And I say they *can* be if we give ourselves the opportunity to heal. When we acknowledge our own pain and realize that it is part, not all of us, we get to take back our power. When we believe that our pain or our dysfunction defines us, we let it rule our lives. But by understanding our story and being compassionate toward ourselves, we can begin stepping into the most loving, compassionate version of ourselves, as well as understanding who we want to be moving forward.

Perhaps you are looking at your story and reflecting on things about yourself that you haven't thought of in a while. Perhaps you are getting some clarity on why you act the way you do.

Keep digging; it will only make you more whole.

Remember, this may or may not be an emotional experience for you. Let it be okay either way.

Also, as a side note, by looking at our story and giving ourselves permission to acknowledge and grieve all the loss experiences of our lives without judgment, we can truly accept other people where they are as well.

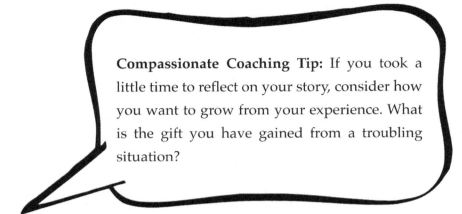

Compassionate Coaching Tip: If you took a little time to reflect on your story, consider how you want to grow from your experience. What is the gift you have gained from a troubling situation?

Honoring each loss experience does not diminish anyone else's losses; it simply allows us to understand ourselves and each other more.

If you pour a handful of salt into a cup of water, the water becomes undrinkable. But if you pour the salt into a river, people can continue to draw the water to cook, wash, and drink. The river is immense, and it has the capacity to receive, embrace, and transform. When our hearts are small, our understanding and compassion are limited, and we suffer. We can't accept or tolerate others and their shortcomings, and we demand that they change. But when our hearts expand, these same things don't make us suffer anymore. We have a lot of understanding and compassion and can embrace others. We accept others as they are, and then they have a chance to transform.

—Thich Nhat Hanh

Chapter 6: Where Do You Live on the Spectrum?

"When you are courting a nice girl, an hour seems like a second. When you sit on a red-hot cinder, a second seems like an hour. That's relativity." — *Albert Einstein*

Everything lives on a spectrum, which is what makes all things relative.

Do you give everyone the benefit of the doubt, or do you think everyone is out to get you?

Do you prefer to talk or listen?

Do you see the glass as full or empty?

Do you trust quickly and easily, or are you slow to trust?

Wherever you fall, it is likely that you would benefit from learning from the other side.

As someone who tends to see the best in people, I have had to learn to be more discerning. A dear friend of mine is similar.

Coming off the heels of a long relationship and a challenging breakup, my friend vulnerably got back out on the dating scene, eager to find her true love and get married.

A few months later, she met a handsome, smart, successful young man who seemed to be exactly what she was looking for. They had a lot in common and quickly fell in love.

Within a couple months of dating, he revealed that he had lied in their initial meeting about his upbringing. While this was clearly a red flag for her, she decided to forgive him and move forward with the relationship. A few months later they became engaged, and the excitement and planning took over.

A month before the wedding, the truth of several other lies was uncovered, but she felt it was too close and she let it go. Six weeks after the wedding the layers of lies, manipulation, and infidelity finally revealed themselves fully. They spent the next year in therapy before the marriage came to an end.

The fact that the man she loved was not who she thought he was broke her heart, but she was also devastated by the fact that she had not listened more to her intuition, and that she hadn't paid attention to the signs that showed up along the way.

After years of therapy and learning the true meaning and practice of self-compassion, she has now learned to lean into her intuition. She has taken responsibility for the person she was and the decisions she made, and she chooses differently now.

Most importantly, she has compassion for the person she was because when you know better, you do better.

Wherever you are, look with curiosity and compassion rather than judgment—and remember to find your center. The growth lies in seeing the spectrum and leaning more toward the places that stretch you.

As it relates to compassion, some people are natural caregivers who can get taken advantage of, while others do whatever they want in the name of boundaries or putting their needs first.

While neither is bad, each side would benefit from leaning toward and learning from the other.

Compassion In Action:
Remember, on the bell curve of compassion, both extremes can lead to disconnection.

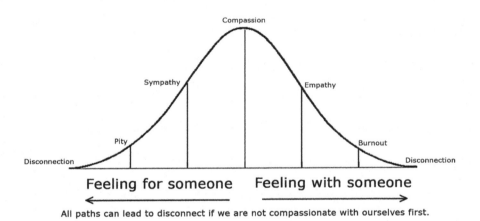

Where do you tend to be? What can you learn from the other side? If you lean toward the pity side of disconnection, practice feeling with others. If you lean toward the burnout side of disconnection, practice safe boundaries.

Chapter 7: Self-Compassion Isn't Self-Esteem

I want to introduce you to one of my favorite researchers in the area of self-compassion, Dr. Kristin Neff. She talks about the difference between self-compassion and self-esteem, and the importance of not comparing ourselves to others. In order to open our hearts to others, we have to begin by opening our hearts to ourselves. By acknowledging that we have a story, it allows us to be more compassionate to the fact that everyone has a story.

One of the biggest challenges we face after experiencing any kind of heartache is that people often tell us our pain is not enough. And if other people aren't telling us that, then we are telling it to ourselves. We think inside of our heads, *Stop complaining . . . so many people in the world have it worse than you. You should feel grateful.* While gratitude is a valuable practice and provides us with great perspective, it can also diminish our experience and allow us to skim past our feelings.

The reason why we participate in this comparison game and this negative self-talk is because we are taught that our self-worth is dependent upon how good we are compared to others.

Self-esteem has been the ultimate marker for psychological health for decades, but the problem with that is it is all about comparing ourselves. "Am I good enough?" is based solely upon how we rank compared to others. And that even includes how sad we are allowed to feel.

According to Dr. Neff, having high self-esteem isn't the problem; the problem is how you achieve high self-esteem. In order to have high self-esteem, we have to consider ourselves special or above average. But how can every person on earth be better than average?

The truth is that the need to be better than others encourages bullying and prejudice, putting others down in order to make yourself feel better.

Since self-esteem is related to achievement and comparison, it often fails us when we need it most. When we are feeling down or when we aren't meeting with success, that internal critic kicks in and we beat ourselves up.

Once we have royally kicked our own butts, like in the story I shared earlier, we present ourselves to the world in a defeated way. How can we feel motivated or be kind to others when we don't know how to be kind to ourselves?

Self-esteem creates more challenges, more isolation, and more need to diminish others, and therefore is not the best tool for healing ourselves or the world around us. However, self-compassion is not a way of judging or self-evaluating; rather, it is a way of relating to ourselves kindlier and accepting ourselves as we are.

According to Neff, the three components of self-compassion are:

1) treating ourselves with kindness rather than judgment, the way we would treat a good friend

2) common humanity—how am I the same as others, rather than different

3) mindfulness—being with what is in the present moment. If we

can acknowledge and accept that we are suffering, we are more able to give ourselves compassion.

These three components are key to self-compassion, but my favorite is the idea of common humanity. Since we have been taught that "laugh and the world laughs with you, cry and you cry alone," we tend to isolate ourselves in our suffering. Many of us proceed through pain pretending to be fine and strong for others, but this self-imposed isolation keeps us from sharing the feelings that unite us as humans. Feeling sad, devastated, frustrated, alone, ashamed, guilty, scared, or even joyful are part of life. We are the opposite of alone; we are one in these feelings.

While what we go through is unique and important, self-compassion helps us acknowledge that what we have been through is nothing to be ashamed of or kept to ourselves. It allows us to embrace our pain and realize that we are not alone. It allows us to accept ourselves and our lives as imperfect, just like every other being on earth. We often think that there is something wrong with us or that we are bad, but separation and self-criticism often lead to depression and anxiety. The reality is that our suffering is what connects us all. Grief is something that we all experience, as no one is immune to feeling the conflicting emotions that make up life.

When it comes to self, the key to choosing love is to pivot away from self-esteem, judging and comparing ourselves to others, and choose self-compassion instead. If we can be kinder to ourselves, we can be kinder to others. If we speak nicely to ourselves, we can speak kindlier to others. And if we can accept that we are all part of the human experience and that this experience is meant to be full of both joy and sorrow, we can stop feeling so isolated in our suffering.

Social media connections like Facebook and Instagram are a modern-day version of the idea of "keeping up with the Joneses," and these sometimes superficial connections are consummate representations of how compare can lead to despair. When we can replace the word jealousy with the word inspiration, and judgment with curiosity, we can begin our journey to healing with personal responsibility. You can also choose your level of engagement based on whether social media leads you down the road of jealousy and self-criticism, or if it is a healthy place for you to be curious and to connect.

Ultimately, it is about finding the balance between honoring your own story as important and unique and allowing other people's stories to give you perspective and gratitude for what you do have. Compassion for yourself can allow you to then be even more compassionate for others.

Compassion In Action Part I: When I am in the mindset of self-hate, self-criticism, or shame, I repeat this mantra to myself (aloud or silently) "I love myself; I am enough." This helps me move back to center every time. If that feels challenging for you, start with, "I am okay as I am." Try this on. The more you practice, the easier it will become.

Compassion In Action Part II: Next time you find yourself feeling jealous, think the thought again and replace it with the word inspired. "I am so inspired by his success," allows you to take empowered action.

Chapter 8: Creating the Space for Compassion

There are numerous times when "I'm fine" feels like a lie, such as on the anniversary of my mom's death, my birthday, my wedding day, the day my daughter was born, or when I see a hummingbird. They are all times when I miss my mom, when I feel a deep pit of sadness, or when I simply don't feel like being chipper.

We all go through days when it is hard to put on a happy face. It's not just when we miss someone who has died, but it also happens when we get into a fight with our significant other, when we feel worried that we aren't going to make ends meet for the month, when we feel stuck in our job, when life isn't going the way we want it to, or when we look in the mirror and don't like what we see.

Since we don't typically live from the inside out—meaning that people don't know what we are going through, and we can't tell what others are going through either—it's important to be intentional about creating the space for compassion.

For example, I was teaching a workshop and on the second day one of the women seemed aloof. I automatically worried that maybe she wasn't enjoying her experience or that she didn't think I was doing a good job. But during our morning check-in, she courageously shared that her husband was being released from the hospital that morning, as he had been hit by a car while biking a few days earlier. As she shared, I realized that her preoccupation had nothing to do with me or our workshop, and that she was worried about her husband. I felt grateful that she shared her situation, and it was an excellent reminder for me to practice what I teach.

Here are a few tools to navigate your relationships with compassion, while also having your emotional needs met.

1. When someone is less than kind, try to imagine what they may be going through. Think of the most generous interpretation of their actions, and give them the benefit of the doubt. The beauty of reacting this way is that instead of anger and frustration, you get to choose compassion and love. Not only is this better for them, but it is also a nicer way for you to relate to the world. Remember, everyone has a story!

2. Tell the truth about yourself. You don't always need to share your most vulnerable feelings with everyone, but when having a close interaction with someone who is affected by your current state, consider sharing a little insight into the way you are acting. For example, when someone asks how you are doing, you may respond, "You know, it's been kind of a hard day. Thank you for asking, though." If you are feeling a bit bolder or are talking to a friend, you could even say, "I'm having a hard day because today is the anniversary of my mom's death. Thanks for asking."

The beauty is when you open up and tell the truth about yourself, a few things happen:

- Your vulnerability often brings you closer to the other person.
- The other person can be understanding and sympathetic about your situation.
- The other person gets to acknowledge how you feel, hopefully without trying to fix it.
- You don't have to pretend to be fine.

3. Ask for what you want or need. Unfortunately—and fortunately—people can't read our minds. When you are having a hard day or moment, tell people what you need. For example, on the last anniversary of my mom's death, I let people know that I was sad and that I missed her. I asked people close to me to share their memories and to go for a walk in her honor. I also asked my husband to be particularly patient and kind to me that day. By asking for what you want, the people in your life are able to support you better. People can't necessarily remember all the dates that are hard or important for us. Set the people in your life up for success by reminding them of challenging dates and telling them what would make that date easier for you.

By giving people the benefit of the doubt, sharing what is going on, and asking for what you need, you set the stage for compassion to flourish for yourself and others, and you are more likely to have your emotional needs met during these moments of inevitable heartache.

Here's an example of a post I made one year on my mom's birthday, which is typically a hard day for me. I didn't make my followers guess; I shared and asked for what I wanted, and the response was amazing.

"Today's my mom's birthday. She would have been 66 years old today. Wow—if she were here, we would probably go for a walk, get a pedicure, and go out to dinner. I will do my best to honor her memory today. If you have any stories about her that you want to share, it is always appreciated. Love you, Mom."

4. If someone tries to "fix" it with a silver lining, politely offer gratitude for their positive intention of trying to help, and say, "All I really need is for you to hear me, acknowledge that this is hard for me, and give me a hug" (or whatever is true for you). Remember, we are all

trying to figure it out. So, if you know what you need, even by default, tell people nicely.

 **Compassion In Action:** Next time someone asks you how you are, pause before you give your auto-response. Then try sharing a little more honestly without feeling like you have to overshare.

Chapter 9: Being Compassionate Starts Within

"Watch your thoughts. They become words. Watch your words. They become deeds. Watch your deeds. They become habits. Watch your habits. They become character. Watch your character. It becomes your destiny." —Lao Tzu

Being compassionate is not something that simply happens easily all at once. It is a practice that we decide to work with so that we can help make the world a better place for others and ourselves. When I am feeling judgmental, frustrated, or upset, I remind myself to put on my Compassion Hat.

Being compassionate starts with your innermost thoughts. By changing your thoughts, you can change your feelings, and thus you can change how you act, react, and respond. If our goal is to *be* compassionate, we must first *think* with compassion, then *feel* with compassion, then *speak* with compassion, and then *act* with compassion.

Let's start with how we can begin thinking compassionately.

Have you ever found yourself in a less than desirable conversation? Perhaps you or someone else is gossiping or speaking negatively about someone else. Do you ever notice that this type of conversation makes you feel worse?

It is hard to be compassionate when we are being nasty in our heads, and that is true whether we are thinking negatively about someone else or ourselves. This can be called a low-vibration state. Resonating at a lower frequency often relates to dissatisfaction, unhappiness, lack, or hatred, whereas high vibration often relates to abundance, love, satisfaction, and happiness—experiences most of us want more of.

So, when I find myself in a low-vibration conversation, judging internally, or around someone who is being mean or judgmental, I have a few tricks to help lift my vibration and find my way back to compassion.

1. I think to myself, *What could this person (whom I am judging) have possibly been through?* This is an exercise in growing our compassion muscle. One remedy is to make up a story in your head about why they could be feeling or acting the way they are.

I think to myself, *What if she caught her boyfriend cheating on her, what if his dog died, what if he found out his dad has a terminal illness, etc.* Then I think about how I would be in the world if one of those scenarios happened to me. And boom! I am immediately back to compassion.

Example: My friend and I were strolling along a trail with my daughter when she waved at a stranger, and he didn't wave back. My friend and I were taken aback, and then I thought, *What if he lost a child and it was just too painful for him to wave back?*

Is it true? I have no idea. But if it is, that sure would make sense, right?

2. I remind myself that it is most likely NOT about me. As much as I love to make things about me, when people are rude or mean (especially strangers), it is most likely because they are experiencing their own difficulties and lashing out.

Example: A man was out shopping for a shirt for his son's funeral. His son's death was only days earlier and he was feeling shocked, devastated, and heartbroken. He found what he was looking for, but he needed a different size. When he asked the sales clerk for the shirt, the young man said he would go look for it. He returned shaking his head, saying that he was sorry but they didn't have it. The man snapped and yelled at the young sales clerk, saying, "I can't believe you don't have what I want. This is awful! I'll never come back." The young man was confused and felt terrible. He thought to himself, *I knew I wasn't meant to be a salesman. I can't do anything right.*

This is a classic example of how misunderstandings happen. Knowing both sides, we can see the man shopping wasn't actually mad at the sales clerk, but rather devastated by his own personal situation. We can also see that the only mistake the sales clerk made was thinking it was about him.

3. Once I am able to let go of it being about me, I recite the mantra, "I am okay just as I am." This brings me back to center and helps me avoid dipping into a negative ego trip.

4. I ask myself, "What can I learn from this experience to make me a better person?"

5. For my last trick, I send them love. I bring attention to my heart and I think to myself, *I hope that whatever they're going through gets better.*

Compassion In Action: When you find yourself thinking negative thoughts, feeling judgmental, or being the recipient of negativity, try out one of the above tricks and you will be well on our way to raising your vibration.

Remember, these things don't happen overnight; you have to practice. With practice, compassionate thoughts, feelings, and actions will become second nature.

It is also important to be kind to ourselves. You, too, have a story.

Sometimes it is easier to be nice to other people. So, once you become good at thinking with compassion, you can turn it around and offer yourself a little compassion too.

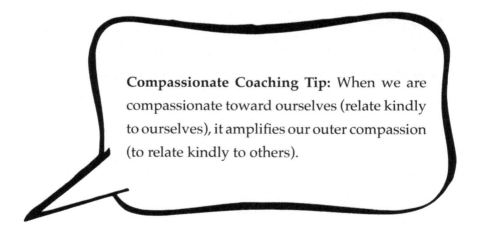

Compassionate Coaching Tip: When we are compassionate toward ourselves (relate kindly to ourselves), it amplifies our outer compassion (to relate kindly to others).

A Note on Compassion Fatigue

If you think about the bell curve of compassion from Chapter 1, compassion fatigue is when we move beyond compassion to empathy (feeling with someone), then into burnout, and at the extreme, disconnection. This tends to happen with people who are highly sensitive and connected to other people's experiences.

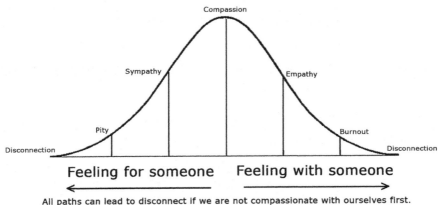

All paths can lead to disconnect if we are not compassionate with ourselves first.

According to Dr. Charles Figley, compassion fatigue is a state experienced by those helping people or animals in distress; it is an extreme state of tension and preoccupation with the suffering of those being helped to the degree that it can create a secondary traumatic stress for the helper.

My secret to feeling compassion for others without letting it negatively affect me is in using my thoughts. Thinking sympathetically may sound like, "*I feel so sad for that person. They are broken . . . what a mess,* or any other such thought implying pity for them or their experience. Thinking empathetically may sound like, *I've felt something like that before and it hurts so badly. I feel heartbroken,* or any other thought

71

or feeling that involves relating so deeply with the other that you feel it immensely yourself.

Thinking compassionately is the balance. I practice using these words internally to prevent burnout: *This person is whole, not broken. I feel sad that they are in pain, and I hope they can move through it and grow from the experience.*

As I respond to people in pain with compassionate thoughts, I allow myself to notice where in my body I feel their pain. Whether it is my heart, my stomach, my head, or elsewhere, I put my hands on the general location and take a deep breath. When I release my breath, I also allow my thoughts and feelings to pass through me. Then I release them with my exhale. (If you do yoga, this may remind you of the warm-up or cool-down period.)

You are welcome to use this simple exercise for now; there are more tools coming later in the book.

PART III: COMPASSIONATE COMMUNICATION

Chapter 10: Compassion Is to Acknowledge, Not Fix

Recently, my husband and I were on vacation, sharing a room with our new baby. The first night, we were lying in our comfy bed and I said, "I really hope she sleeps well tonight."

Aaron responded, "Don't worry so much, she'll be fine."

I immediately got defensive because he tried to fix what I was feeling. He had good intentions and wanted to help me, but he unintentionally diminished my feelings.

What could he have said instead?

It is both to my husband's advantage and perhaps, at times, to his detriment, that I'm exceedingly open with my feelings and my communications. My response was, "I know you're trying to help, but telling me not to worry doesn't take away my anxiety. Instead you might say, "I hope she sleeps well too. I know sleep is really important to you, and it's normal to worry when traveling abroad with a young baby."

Acknowledging and normalizing my feelings would have been more helpful and would have kept the communication open.

When we try to fix, a few things can happen:

1. The person's feelings are diminished, which can cause them to shut down.

2. The person can become defensive, which can cause them to shut down.

3. On rare occasions, the person is open to the suggestion.

In my case, telling me that what I was feeling was unnecessary wasn't helpful. However, in that instance he could first acknowledge my feelings, and then offer a practical solution like getting up early with her or helping during the night. A suggestion can be helpful *if* we are acknowledged and validated first.

Fortunately for me, I'm in a relationship where I can actually say, "Can you please say this instead?" And even though it may seem a little silly for him to simply repeat what I said, I definitely felt more supported and heard. And after I give him the script, he usually files it away and almost always does a better job supporting me the next time. With the lines of communication open, I don't build any resentment. Win, win.

The difference between acknowledging and fixing is that fixing shuts people down, while acknowledging keeps the communication open. Compassion is all about trying to understand other people's stories, and acknowledgement is the first step. We can't even begin to understand their story if we are in the midst of trying to fix them.

Now that you understand the difference between acknowledging and fixing, I want to offer another level to the conversation of fixing. "Wait," you say. "I thought you said we aren't supposed to try to fix other people's pain." Good! You were paying attention.

However, it isn't always easy to keep our opinions to ourselves, so here's a good way to offer a solution with respect and grace, and to ease the possibility of intrusion.

Ask permission to offer your thoughts. For example, you may say,

"May I offer you a thought / my opinion / another option?" or "May I ask a clarifying question?" The key here is the *May I . . .* Typically, others respond well to it because they can always say no. If the answer is no, it is best to respect their request.

"Can I share a story that seems relevant?" The danger with this one is that you have to make sure you avoid "story stealing." Story stealing is when we talk about our own story, and it actually ends up taking away from what the other person is saying rather than adding to it. This is usually unintentional, but it is quite common. At this point, I want to remind you not to say things like, "I know exactly how you feel" or "Yeah, I know how you feel. One time my . . ." These generally lend themselves to story stealing.

"Can I tell you what's coming up for me (what I'm thinking and feeling), and you can tell me if it sounds true for you?" Again, remember to wait for the green light before sharing.

> **Compassionate Coaching Tip:** If you are going to share something you have experienced to help validate the other person, use the word similar rather than same. Similar allows for them to feel like they are not alone, but it still recognizes uniqueness. For example, when someone tells me that they lost their mom in a tragic accident, I may say something like, "Gosh, I can't imagine what this has been like for you. I similarly lost my mom tragically and it was devastating for me. I am so sorry you have to go through this." Then I am quiet and let them share what they are experiencing.

Chapter 11: The Four Most Common Responses to Grief (That Are Surprisingly NOT Compassionate)

We are all grievers. You may think you are not yet a griever because you haven't lost a loved one. Well, at the Grief Recovery Institute, we define grief as "the conflicting feelings caused by the end of, or change in, a familiar pattern of behavior."

What that means is that if you have experienced a transition in your life, you have experienced grief. If you have gone through a breakup or divorce, gone away to college, lost a job, become a new parent or empty nester, lost your role as a caregiver, gotten married, or any other major change (including the death of someone important to you), you have experienced grief.

Each of us has experienced pain at some point in our lives. Yet when others face tough times, we usually have no idea what to do or say when they tell us their troubles.

I often hear people say, "No one feels like I feel," or "If I tell people how I feel, they may think I'm crazy or may not want to be around me." Even though we have all been through something—a crumbled relationship, losing someone dear, a move, a rejection, etc.—we often feel alone in our painful experiences.

The truth is that people often don't know how to relate to your emotions because they don't know how to relate to their own. We aren't given tools as a society to deal with the sad stuff. We are expected to feel good most or all of the time. When you say, "How are you?" the most common response is "Fine, how are you?" It immediately takes the spotlight off how you are doing and puts it on the other.

When we do have something going on in our lives that isn't so great, and we have the courage to tell the truth, we are often hit with the following four mechanical responses. Before we get into what to say, let's address what NOT to say and why these comments may be painful to the receiver.

The platitude. A platitude is a remark, especially one with moral content, that has been used too often to be interesting or thoughtful. While it can be helpful to say "I'm sorry" when you have done something wrong, many of my clients have shared that "I'm sorry" doesn't always feel appropriate, and can even imply a guilt that is unneeded. Other platitudes can be "Good things come to those who wait," "It was meant to be," or "Forgive and forget."

The quick fix. The quick fix is common in our society because we are geared toward problem-solving. These statements include comments like "You'll find someone else" or "You'll get a new job."

The optimist. The optimist is a sister to the quick fix. This person tries to make it better by sharing how it could have been worse. It often sounds like "At least you have other children," "You can get a new dog," or "Think of all the time you had together . . ."

The story stealer. This person is trying to relate to you, but in doing so they tell you, "I know exactly how you feel" and (often) proceed by telling you their own story. At the Grief Recovery Institute, we say that no two losses are the same. Even if it looks the same from the outside, everyone grieves differently. Comparing your loss can sometimes come across as disrespectful, and even insulting.

As Allison James from the Grief Recovery Institute wrote in a helpful article, "When grievers do build up the courage to share their emotions, sympathetic friends usually say, 'I know how you feel.' That well-meaning phrase robs grievers of the opportunity to openly share their feelings. . . . Let grievers talk openly and freely without sharing your own experiences, correcting them, or interrupting."

What all of these phrases have in common is that they fall on the "fixing" rather than the "acknowledging" end of the spectrum. They're aimed at trying to make it better, rather than trying to understand. To show compassion to someone in pain, it's important they feel heard, understood, and validated, not like their feelings are being brushed aside.

We say these mechanical things because we don't know what else to say. We don't know how to respond when people are sad. If we don't have any tools to support others during the dark moments, we simply say what other people have said to us, even though we don't necessarily appreciate those words.

As much as I hate to admit it, I have been the platitude-user, the quick-fixer, the optimist, and the story stealer. If this describes you too, be compassionate toward yourself. Most of us struggle with finding the "right thing to say," and that is why I am going to share some new strategies with you.

Before we get into the tools to shift how you respond more compassionately to grief, let's cover the six myths of grief and how they, too, show up in our communication.

Chapter 12: Let's Talk More About Grief

As I mentioned earlier, after my mom died, I thought I had to be strong. I only cried by myself or at night with my husband. No one ever saw me "break down" because I was ashamed and worried what others would think. I was concerned that I would be a burden, and I was fearful they wouldn't love me, or if they did, they would pity me.

One day, about nine months after her death—busy being strong for my dad, my brother, and everyone else—I finally admitted to my dad that I was devastated and that I missed Mom. He said, "There you are." I was confused. He shared that he had been worried about me because I hadn't shown any emotion since my mom died. I told him I was trying to be strong for him, to which he responded, "You don't have to be strong for me, Laura. You're my baby."

And that was the end of pretending I was fine.

You see, the idea of "being strong" is merely a myth that exists in our culture about grief. Many of us have been taught, both consciously and subconsciously, to say certain things to people experiencing grief that actually aren't helpful—and now you get a chance to learn more about these phrases. Moreover, if you are anything like me, you may simply act out these myths because you think that's "what you are supposed to do."

These six myths about grief from the Grief Recovery Institute give incredible insight into how to word your compassionate responses, highlighting how these myths often perpetuate communication that doesn't serve others or ourselves.

Let's cover each myth first and how it shows up, and then we'll talk about what to say instead.

Myth 1: Don't feel bad. People don't want you to feel bad because they want you to feel good. That's *nice* and it comes from a good place, but the challenge comes from the fact that we *do* feel bad sometimes. Sometimes we are sad, confused, lonely, angry, and frustrated. Those feelings are valid. When we say something like, "Don't worry, it's all going to be okay," we are trying to be helpful, but it can diminish what the person is saying or feeling. Further, the person may defensively respond that we don't, in fact, know how things will turn out. Since this is factual, this false prognostication is not valuable.

Myth 2: Replace the loss. We often use this one around pet loss, the end of a relationship, or even a job loss. You hear and say things like, "Don't worry, you'll find a new position," or "He wasn't that great anyway." People like to say that you can get a new dog, job, boy.friend, car, etc., and while it may be true on an intellectual level, it's not that helpful to someone who is suffering in that moment.

Myth 3: Grieve alone. This myth has been detrimental because it encourages isolation and stuffing emotions down. It's important to distinguish between wanting to be alone and feeling like you need to be alone because you don't want to burden someone else. Having the support and love of others can be therapeutic and allow you to see that while our experiences are unique, we are having feelings that are universal. In words, this can sound like, "Call me if you need me," "Your mother needs to be alone," or "Go to your room if you're going to cry like that."

Myth 4: Time heals all wounds. This is another cliché that simply isn't true. Similar to "It's all going to be okay," this expression entails omniscient hope. Time itself does not create healing; it takes all possibility out of our hands because we can't control time. When we take action, like participating in the Grief Recovery Method, we are making a choice to heal. Then time can do its job.

Myth 5: Keep busy. This is similar to "time heals all wounds" because it insinuates that if you stay busy long enough, time will heal you, but this isn't necessarily going to prove true for everyone. At the end of a busy day, whatever loss or challenge you are facing is still there. If you don't face your pain and difficult unresolved feelings, you can't heal or grow. "Staying busy" encourages you to continue avoiding.

Myth 6: Be strong. This is one of the most common things people say that is *not* helpful. What *be strong* means to me is "pretend you're fine," which is exactly what I was doing wrong in my own grief years ago. This isn't helpful because it encourages someone to put on a happy face for others so that they don't have to deal with that person's emotions. This myth causes isolation and forces someone to lie or suppress their true feelings.

Understanding these myths and misinformation about grief are vital to upgrading our language and communication in response to loss and other challenges.

Think about some of the worst things people have said to you or some of the above myths you have heard or even said. Sometimes knowing what to say is most obvious when we first think about what *not* to say.

It's okay if you have said the "wrong" thing before. Because you didn't do anything with the intention to harm, you should exercise self-compassion. You aren't here to be hard on yourself or judgmental;

you are here to learn and become a more educated, compassionate communicator.

In the following chapter, we'll get into the nitty gritty of how to communicate compassionately.

Compassion In Action: Describe one situation where you have experienced grief that others or you yourself responded to your grief with one or more of the six myths of grief? What was the outcome. In the next Chapter, I'll describe what the person, including you, could have done or said differently. You can then imagine how the outcome could have looked different.

Chapter 13: Compassion Sounds Like . . . (aka What to Say)

"He was a mess."

"She was falling apart."

"I just broke down."

"He was mental."

What do all of these have in common? They imply that it isn't okay to feel our feelings. Because they are common expressions we use without thinking about what they mean, they ultimately convey judgments of ourselves or others for having a natural reaction to life's challenges.

Feeling our feelings is necessary for moving through the pain of loss and life's transitions. That's why it's important to shift our language away from self-criticism and judgment. I want you to start noticing and avoiding language like:

I (or he/she/they) fell apart.

I was a mess.

I broke down.

The sooner we accept ourselves and others, even in our language, the more easily we can move through our pain.

Things to say instead are:

1) I was sad.

2) I was devastated by the circumstances.

3) I am grieving.

4) I feel heartbroken.

I encourage my clients to remember that tears are better out than in, and that when they embrace their feelings, they are one step closer to wholeness. Peace comes from unblocking our resistance, discontinuing the repression of feelings, and allowing ourselves to feel even when it seems scary.

If you or someone you love is afraid to "let it out," have them contact a Certified Grief Recovery Specialist or a licensed professional to process these feelings.

Compassionate Coaching Tip: Try using the word *and* rather than the word *but* when someone shares something with you, even if you have a different opinion. *But* can prevent the person who is sharing from opening up further because it can discount what was said before. *And* allows you to contribute to what's already been shared. For example, someone rhetorically asks, "Would you be able to come over?" Now, feel the difference in these responses.

"Yes, and would it be okay if I came over tomorrow? Tonight I have a commitment." Or "Yes, but I can't today."

Notice that they are saying the same thing, and yet the first one creates greater possibilities.

"But" is not always discounting or negative—it can be explanatory or help someone process why they do something or feel a certain way. For example, if I say, "I wanted to cry, but I didn't want people to pity me," I'm not discounting crying, but rather simply explaining why I felt I couldn't cry.

Let's Review

Okay, now let's do a quick review of the four most common responses in challenging situations and the six myths of grief and how they show up in ways we want to avoid.

Compassionate Coaching Tip: Remember even experienced users of compassion make mistakes. As I mentioned earlier in the book, compassion is a practice. Do the best you can to create awareness around these "Unhelpful Expressions", and be compassionate toward yourself when you forget.

The "Unhelpful Expressions":
Try not to say things that are intellectually true but not helpful emotionally.[10]

---

10   Grief Recovery Handbook

- If I were to say, "I had a miscarriage," you would NOT say, "You're young, at least you can have another child." While this may be true intellectually, it is emotionally painful and unhelpful.

Try not to use the words "at least" or other diminishing words when responding to someone sharing their pain, challenge, trauma, or drama. Anything following the words *at least* can diminish someone's feelings.

"At least they're in a better place." The person is probably thinking, *No, not to me they aren't.*

"At least you didn't have any children with him." The person may be thinking, *How do you know I didn't want to?*

"At least you can find someone better." The person may think, *What if I don't want to find someone else?*

"No offense, but . . ." is another diminishing expression. Usually whatever you are about to say is offensive. Avoid it.

"I love him to death, but . . ." usually means you are going to say something you don't like.

Don't offer platitudes or clichés like:[11]

"Give it time."

"Stay busy."

"You'll find someone else."

"That job sucked anyway."

"Call me if you need me."

"You've got to be strong for . . ."

---

11   Grief Recovery Handbook

"Pick yourself up by your bootstraps."

"Suck it up.

"It's time to move on."

"You should be over it by now."

Don't "story-steal" or compare stories[12] as better, worse, or the same. One of my students, Mar Feder, put it best when she said, "Every loss deserves to be honored with grief."

"You think that's bad? Listen to what happened to me . . ."

"My friend had something way worse happen. You're lucky you . . ."

"That's nothing, I . . ."

I am sure you have said or heard one, if not all, of these. They are rarely, if ever, helpful, and these little words may be the reason you haven't heard from someone in a while.

You may be thinking, *Laura, you just "took away" everything I have to say in these circumstances!*

Keep in mind that all of the above responses and myths have one common theme: they are trying to fix. You don't need to fix someone who is grieving. You simply need to listen deeply first and then validate.

Here's what to do and say instead:

1. Listen deeply.

2. Be present.

3. Acknowledge the person's feelings, and try to recognize their perspective as what is true for them.

4. Validate the person's experience and let them know they are not alone.

---

12   Grief Recovery Method

5. Be genuinely curious about what he or she is feeling, judgment aside.

6. Tell the truth about yourself and sincerely feel with them. For example, "I wish I knew what to say . . . I feel so sad you have to go through this. I'm here."

7. Find the words and body language that feel authentic for you. I typically take a deep breath, nod my head or touch my heart, and say, "That sucks" or "I am so sorry you have to go through this. I've been in a similar situation, and I know it's rough."

People often ask how I feel about the phrases "My condolences," or "I'm sorry for your loss." These two phrases are fairly neutral. Most people are not offended by either; however, they can create disconnect because they may be considered clichéd or scripted. Better than "I'm sorry for your loss" is adding the specific loss. For example, "I'm sorry to hear about your mom."

If you have time to go deeper and it's clear the griever wants to discuss, ask, "What happened?"[13] or "Tell me about her." When they tell you, your response can be:

"I can't imagine what that's been like for you."[14]

"I wish it were different for you." Or "I wish that hadn't happened to you."

"My heart hurts for you."

"Thank you for sharing that with me." Gratitude is beneficial because it lets them know that it is safe to open up to you. Depending on the situation, you can ask questions that show love and care rather than judgment, but I will return to that later.

After each of the above, I recommend that you take a couple breaths and stay quiet long enough to listen to what the person sharing has

---

13   Grief Recovery Certification Training

14   Grief Recovery Certification Training

to say. Make sure they feel comfortable, assured that you are there to listen and not judge or offer unsolicited advice.

A more advanced technique that we use at the Grief Recovery Institute is phrasing feeling words, such as "sad," "angry," or "frustrated" as questions. I call this *fishing*. This entails throwing a line out with a feeling word with a clear question on the end.

See the difference between "You must be sad," and "Were you sad?"

When a feeling is offered with a question, it gives the other person a chance to correct you, and you are getting more clarity into how they actually feel. In other words, you are fishing to find what is true for them. e.g., Were you frustrated? Mad? Relieved? Scared?

This technique is most useful when the griever is telling you a factual story and you are trying to arrive at the feeling part. It is not necessary when they are sharing their feelings with you, but you can ask a clarifying question to get to the core of that feeling.

Compassionate Coaching Tip: These techniques work beautifully for texting too. If someone shares something personal over text, you can use the fishing technique to find out more. For example, they text you that they are breaking up with their boyfriend. You can respond, "Relieved? Heartbroken? Shocked?" Then no matter where they fall, they can correct you, and by offering the spectrum of emotions, you are not assuming how they feel. When texting, you can also always follow up with "Want to talk about it (later)?"

You can also respond with:

1. "Thank you so much for sharing with me."

2. "Your feelings are totally valid."

3. "It's natural to feel this way."

4. "I can see where you're coming from."

5. "That makes sense."

If you want to share a personal experience that feels related you can ask, "May I share a personal experience that feels relevant?"

If you are going to share, remember that it is about the other person in this moment, not you.

As I mentioned earlier in the book, it is important that you don't compare. Another communication that destroys compassion and connection is comparing.

By comparing you can either diminish or isolate the other person's experience or feelings. It's diminishing when you say, "At least you still have your other leg." And you isolate others when you say, "Your loss is the worst and you'll never recover." Of course, you have good intentions to be positive or want them to feel like their loss is important, but you can end up causing more harm than good.

I had a client who shared that when she confronted her mom about her verbal abuse, her mom would say, "You don't know what abuse is." While my client felt compassion for her mother because she was also abused as a child, this response diminished my client's experience and feelings about what she went through.

You definitely don't want to put people you love in a box that says, "You will *never* be okay again." Even if they feel that way, we don't want to amplify it.

The truth is, people are incredibly resilient and can overcome almost anything with the right resources and mindset. But before anyone can recover, we have to acknowledge the pain.

It is also important to know that other people may say to you, "At least my mom is in a better place," "At least we didn't have kids together," or "At least we had twenty years together." If you recall, these are some of the expressions I advised you not to use earlier because of their diminishing qualities. However, if the person grieving proposes a silver lining to their situation, let it be. We don't need to tell them, "Sorry, I learned that those 'at-least' statements aren't helpful." They can say whatever they want to help them cope with their own experience, unless it sounds self-harming.

For example: "At least I had a lot of time with them . . . but now I have nothing else to live for." If someone you are talking to says something that indicates suicidal or self-harming thoughts, please do not take these comments lightly. Utilize the resources in the back of the book and seek immediate professional help.

Some people may say things like, "I'm fine," "I'm staying busy," "I have to be strong for . . .," or "I should be over it by now." Your response in this case is up to your intuition and comfort with the person. If you feel it is appropriate, you can try sharing something you have learned.

For example, if they say, "I have to be strong for my kids," you could respond: "It's so kind that you're trying to be strong for your kids. I just want you to know that you don't have to be strong for me"; or "It's so considerate that you want to be strong for your kids. I also feel that when you express your feelings, it will give them permission to do so as well."

You can also say, "It's okay to be sad," because you want to normalize whatever feelings they are having. Whatever they are going through, it is normal and natural to feel sad, mad, frustrated, etc. Instead of encouraging false or feigned strength, offer gratitude to the griever for allowing themselves to be vulnerable with you. Say, "Thank you for sharing with me." It is actually stronger to be vulnerable than it is to seem strong.

If they say, "I should be over it by now," you can ask, "What makes you feel that way?" If they say that someone in their life thinks this way, you can say, "It's really up to you. You have to take care of yourself. While this person probably has good intentions, if you aren't over it yet, you're fine to feel that way."

If they say that they wish they were over it by now, you can ask if they want any resources to help them process their grief better. If they say they do, you can refer them to my website, www.laurajack.com, the Grief Recovery Institute, www.griefrecoverymethod.com, or any of the other listings in the Resources section at the back of this book.

To offer continued support, the best way to ask is, "Do you mind if I call and check in on you from time to time?" This assures them that they are not alone and takes the pressure off of them to ask for help.

> **Compassionate Coaching Tip:** Make sure you actually follow up if they say yes. Ask them what method (and frequency) of communication works best for them: a weekly phone call, a monthly coffee date, an email on occasion, a daily text, etc. Also, honor your own boundaries and know what kind of time and energy you have available.

Compassion In Action: A lot of people feel selfish if they are taking care of themselves, but it is your job as a compassionate warrior to encourage self-care. You can ask, "What have you been doing to take care of yourself lately?"

Common Scenarios Where Compassionate Communication Is Helpful

I want to point out the difference between having a deep conversation with a close friend and having a superficial conversation with an acquaintance or a stranger. I will start with some basic guidelines for having a surface-level conversation, and then I will move into some more advanced topics and questions for closer relationships.

Remember, the best way to begin compassionate communication is by reminding yourself that everyone has a story behind the face they are showing the world.

Scenario 1:

You are talking to a coworker, acquaintance, or stranger and they tell you that they are getting divorced. The immediate reaction is typically going to come from our map of the world or our perspective on divorce. One of the most compassionate things you can do is not assume you know how they feel. Instead of saying, "I'm so sorry" or

"That's great news," you can gently say, "Are you relieved? Sad? How has it been for you lately?" By being curious and offering a variety of feelings, you give them an opportunity to answer honestly.

Remember to acknowledge and validate. This may sound like, "I hear you" or "I see what you're saying. Your feelings are valid."

- Remember, you can tell the truth about yourself without making it about you. "I can't imagine what that's like for you" (because you can't—every experience is unique). If you have your own story, you can say, "I know our experiences are different, but I just want you to know that when I got divorced, I had a lot of mixed emotions."

- If you have time, you can ask curiously and with care, "How is this affecting you on a daily basis?" and then give them a chance to answer. If they say they would rather not answer, that's okay. No need to take it personally.

- As a compassionate friend, you can ask, "What nice thing have you done for yourself lately?" If they haven't, encourage them to do some self-care.

Scenario 2:

You are talking to a friend, and they tell you they have been diagnosed with cancer or some other loss-of-health experience. Again, the immediate reaction is typically going to come from our perspective. In this case, it is important that you share your truth without making it about you. Here are some things you can try:

- Touch your hand to your chest (whatever feels comfortable for you) and say, "I am so sorry to hear that. What terrible news." Remember this isn't about pity or feeling sorry for them; it is about compassion and feeling into their experience.

- I would then say something like, "What do you know so far? Is it serious?" then listen deeply, without judgment or the need to fix.

- You can ask with curiosity and care, "Are you scared?" or you can say something like, "I can't imagine all the different feelings you're having."

- Remember, it is always okay to say, "I have no idea what to say . . . I wish this weren't true." You can also ask if a hug would be helpful. (If they say no, respect it, and don't take it personally.)

- It is okay if you tear up or feel emotional. They probably appreciate the fact that you care. It is also okay if you don't. Just don't fall to the ground and make it about your feelings instead of theirs. It is about them when they have shared something intimate with you. When you are talking to someone who is there to listen and support you, then you can focus on your feelings.

- This is also a good time to ask who knows the news and if you should keep it confidential. When people tell me that they haven't told anyone or very few people, and ask if I can keep it to myself, I respond with, "Yes, it's your experience to share, not mine. This is between us unless you tell me it isn't."

- I always offer appreciation for people sharing their most vulnerable feelings or updates with me. It is a big deal and can truly bring you closer. By offering gratitude, you can also avoid fixing or coming up with a solution.

- In this particular situation it can also be helpful to say, "Would you mind if I check in on you and ask how you're doing from time to time?" Then you can follow up with them and find out about their progress—again from curiosity and care.

- Whatever you do, do not share a similar situation of someone else you knew who died from what your friend is diagnosed with. That is clearly not helpful in this case. You are here to be a compassionate listener.

- Again, try not to use any "at leasts." You don't want to say anything along the lines of "At least it's only stage 2 cancer, it could be stage 3 or 4." Whatever way you slice it for them, it's devastating. Don't diminish it.

Scenario 3:

Someone you are very close to is going through a challenging time. Perhaps, they are getting divorced, found out that they have cancer, or have lost someone they love. What do you do as their closest person?

- "I want to be here for you, and I am, but I have no idea what I'm doing. I know you don't necessarily know what I should do, but if you have some idea of how I can best support you, can you please tell me?"

- "When you know, tell me. I want to be as involved as possible with supporting you."

- "Do you want me to help you come up with solutions, or do you want me to listen?"

- "Do you want a hug?"

- "Can I come over and sit with you? We don't have to talk unless you want to."

Scenario 4:

Your best friend tells you they are thinking about getting a divorce. What do you say?

- "I'm so sad to hear that you guys are struggling." (if that is true for you)

- Avoid saying, "He/She is such a jerk. I'm so glad you finally see it." You never know if they will get back together or try to work it out. If so, you will be the friend who gets kicked to the curb because you weren't supportive.

- "Do you want me to be the friend who reminds you of your vows and supports you that way? Or do you want me to be the friend who is blindly on your side and says 'What a jerk?'"

- You can ask caring questions like, "Have you told your parents?" "Have you told your kids?" "How did they react?" "Was that hard?"

Remember, compassionate communication DOES NOT:

- Fix

- Diminish

- Isolate

Compassionate communication DOES:

- Listen deeply

- Acknowledge

- Validate

- Accept

Compassionate Coaching Tip: Use how and what rather than why. Why can trigger defensiveness. Feel the difference: "Why did you do that?" versus "What caused that?" One feels judgmental and one feels curious. Try it out.

Compassion In Action: Actively listen to a problem of a friend or family member. What are you first reactions to their story and why? Using compassionate communication, do you change your responses to their narrative?

Handling Complicated Communications in Social Media

These days, the most common place to find out about people's devastating, exciting, or life-changing news is through social media. People like to share things like, "After years of trying, what felt like endless heartbreak, hundreds of injections, pills, scans, and appointments, we can finally announce we have a little one joining us next year. Infertility is not fun and a lot of people suffer in silence.

Facebook announcements can be challenging to see when you're having a hard time getting pregnant."

The following are some ideas about how to respond with compassion:

- "Thank you for sharing. I'm so happy for you, and I'm grateful that you're willing to be vulnerable."

- "Thank you for sharing. I'm so excited for you!"

- "I can't believe I didn't know what was going on for you. I'm so happy to hear that you're pregnant! I'm so sorry, though, to hear that it's been such a struggle, and I appreciate your honest message. It really reminds us that we don't always know what's going on under the surface." (Write a personal message or make a phone call if you consider the person more than a Facebook friend.)

Here is another unfortunate but common social media experience: "The recent tragedy has hit close to home for my family. I/we were very close friends with one of the victims. Please pray for us."

- This is a great opportunity to share a loving story about the person who died if you knew them.

- You could say something like, "Thank you for sharing. My heart aches for your family. Sending peace and love during this challenging time."

- You can make a comment like, "How devastating for all the families and friends involved in this tragedy. Sending love to you, my friend."

- If your truth is, "There are no words for this terrible tragedy," then say that. And you can add, "I'm so sorry to hear that you/ your family is suffering."

If the scenario is someone sharing that they have been diagnosed with a disease, you can use any of the suggestions above in written form. I always start with "Thank you for sharing," and then I add:

"I can't imagine what that's been like for you."

"I wish it were different for you."

"My heart hurts for you."

"Please share updates as things evolve."

If it is someone you know more than as a Facebook friend, you can send a personal message. Here is one that I sent to an old friend who had been diagnosed with cancer:

I just want to thank you. Thank you for sharing yourself with us. Thank you for being brave and honest instead of "being strong," which I believe is just pretending to be fine when you aren't.

I feel sad and angry that you have to go through this . . . I can't imagine how you are feeling. If it is okay with you, I would love to reach out to you periodically to see how you are feeling, what you are doing, and what is going well—and not well—if you want to share.

I know I haven't been a part of your life for a while, but I want you to know I care about you. You were always there for me, and I would appreciate the opportunity to be there for you now. Sending you love, support, and a big hug, Laura

Remember, these are my suggestions, but if you put on your Compassion Hat and speak from the heart, I'm sure you will find the right words for your situation.

The truth is, there are countless scenarios of people sharing the most intimate details of their lives through social media. If you find yourself upset or frustrated that they didn't tell you personally, remember that sometimes people share on social media because it is a quick and less confrontational way to announce things to friends, family, and acquaintances. Even though it is clearly not anonymous, it can be easier to hide behind the screen than to call each friend to share big news.

One of the hardest parts about my mom's death was having to share it with the people in my life who mattered most. Fortunately for me, by the time I got back to the States, almost everyone in my life already knew. It was actually a huge relief that I didn't have to be the one to share.

If you find out about important news on Facebook or some other social media source, be compassionate. Try not to take it personally that they didn't specifically tell you. They wanted you to know on some level or they wouldn't have shared. If this is someone important to you, take the next step and reach out to them personally using some of the strategies you have learned here.

If it is someone you don't know well, and you find yourself thinking, *Ugh . . . why are they sharing in social media?* put on your Compassion Hat and remember that one of the strengths of social media is allowing you to vulnerably share and receive support. As much as I have mixed feelings about social media, this particular aspect can be powerful to combat the myth that it's better to grieve alone.

When You're Scared to Ask the Hard Questions

One day after work, I went over to a friend's house for dinner. We were hanging out, listening to music, and chopping vegetables for dinner, and I said, "Steven, how are you?"

His mostly kidding response surprised me. He said, "Damn, Laura, why do you always have to ask such hard questions?!"

Believe it or not, "How are you?" is one of the deepest, hardest questions you can ask someone. If you ask and truly want the answer, it can be scary for both you and them. When we ask hard questions, we need time, energy, and the capacity to listen to the answer (and ideally know how to respond). So often, we simply don't ask.

"I'm fine," is what people say to avoid "getting emotional" or sharing something that someone "can't handle." And we're afraid to ask people hard questions for fear that we won't know how to respond. As grievers, we are afraid to answer because then we might be vulnerable.

If you know someone is going through a hard time, instead of asking, "How are you?" (because they are most likely not doing well), ask:

- "How is your day going?" (this recognizes that each day is different)
- "Has this been a good day or a challenging day?" (this allows them to be honest)
- "Have you done anything nice for yourself today?" (this is reinforcing self-care)
- "What's going on for you today?"

As you learn what to say and how to ask, commit to doing so every chance you get.

For generations we've been passing down the same message of not to feel, that expressing emotions is the same as being weak, and it has created an emotion-phobic society.

Don't cry. Laugh and the world laughs with you, cry and you cry alone.

What are we supposed to do with this when we are experiencing the roller coaster of emotions that life brings?

We have to start making it okay to feel. We have to stop being afraid of our feelings, both good and bad. Because when we feel great, we think, Is it okay that I'm so happy when so many people are struggling?

Compassion In Action: When someone asks "How are you?" and you want to be more honest, you can say, "You know, I am not having the best day; thanks for asking, though." If you don't want to say more, you don't have to, and you can say, "I'd rather not talk about it right now." It is just nice to practice honesty. You can also say, "It's been a rough few months, and I am taking it one day at a time."

And when we feel awful we think, What's wrong with me?

It's time to understand that this is what it's like to be human. We feel good, we feel bad, and everything in between. Accepting our own emotions is half the battle.

Having some self-compassion will allow us to also accept other people as they are.

Chapter 14: Compassionate Communication Without Words

I remember a time when I was hysterically crying and my friend gave me a hug. His breathing mimicked mine for a few moments and then he slowed his breath. I matched him, and I began to calm down and feel better. Later, when I arrived home after hearing the news about my mom, my dad was in a similar position of hysterical crying, and I did the same thing my friend had done for me. It felt so good to have a tool I could use without having to use any words at all.

Rapport is simply a friendly relationship, and according to Merriam-Webster it means, "a relation marked by harmony, conformity, accord, or affinity."

Something I heard that has stayed with me is that we are attracted to "like kind." What that means in this context is that human beings who are suffering relate more easily with others who have suffered. As we have all suffered some kind of loss, we are all of like kind because we are human. Because of this, building rapport is not only possible, but can be easy.

We are drawn toward others who are like us, but we also want people to know that our experience is unique and different. Oddly enough, we spend our first eighteen-plus years conforming, trying to fit in and be the "same" as others, and then we spend the rest of our lives striving to differentiate ourselves.

We all want to be the same and to be different—meaning, we want to know that we are not alone AND we also want people to know that our experience is different. At the Grief Recovery Institute, we talk about the importance of uniqueness and not comparing. But we as humans also feel isolated, like no one in the world has ever felt what we have. So while our experiences are unique, and no one can completely understand what you are going through, feeling hurt, heartache, pain, loneliness, guilt, shame, longing, abandonment, anxiety, and sadness are feelings that we as humans all get to/have to feel.

Let's circle back to building rapport, a friendly relationship marked by harmony, and how it relates to body language and thus acting compassionately.

When it comes to rapport and acting compassionately, there are a few simple tools that you can start with.

1. Offer good eye contact. You don't have to stare without blinking, but when you look at someone in the eyes, it lets them know:
   - You care.
   - You are paying attention.
   - You aren't afraid to be there with them.

2. Have your body language match your words. If you are saying you care, face them and look at them.

3. Keep an open posture. If you are sitting or standing, generally keep your arms and legs uncrossed (see an exception to this in the next section about matching). When your arms or legs are crossed or you are facing away from the person, it sends a communication that you are closed off.

4. Stay present. Try to stay with them and focus on the words they are saying. If you look away or zone out, they will likely shut

down and feel as if you don't care.

5. If you accidentally become distracted, zone out, or find yourself thinking about something else, tell them. You can say, "Hey, I really want to hear what you have to say . . . I got distracted for a second. Do you mind repeating the last thing you said?" By telling the truth and letting them know you care, you can almost always regain rapport.

Advanced Rapport Building Techniques

If you are ready to go a little deeper, here is a more advanced tip for building rapport and acting compassionately.

Matching[15] is a technique used to build rapport. It means using the same or similar body language and micro-behaviors of the other person.

Remember, conformity is in the definition of rapport. By matching the other person's body language and other behaviors—not in a mocking way but in a conscious, loving way—they will feel more heard and you will both feel more connected.

Here are some of the behaviors you can practice matching:

- Posture
- Hand gestures
- Head tilt
- Facial expression
- Energy level
- Vocal qualities (tone, rhythm, volume)

---

15   Transformational Coaching Method

- Breathing rate

- Key language phrases

Again, you are matching, not mimicking.

To match someone:

- Observe them.

- Slowly move into similar positions.

- Adjust your tone of voice.

- Be similar.

Once you become skilled at matching, the person will likely not notice, but they will feel the rapport. Again, this is done with love and the intention of building connection, not to be offensive.

This may sound strange to you, but you already build rapport regularly. As humans, we match the behavior of babies and animals to connect with them—when we hear them make certain noises or gestures, we do the same to help them feel safe. We actually do it without thinking; in fact, you are probably already unconsciously doing this with other adults. Once you master the art of matching, it will become second nature.

The next step is pacing and leading, which are techniques used to positively influence someone else's behaviors. Pacing means matching their movements, breath, and other micro-behaviors. Once you are pacing with them and matching their behaviors, you can try leading. The above story of my friend breathing with me is an example of pacing and leading.

A few examples of ways this can be helpful are:

- When someone is physically upset, you can meet them where they are with faster breath, similar facial expression, and high energy. Once you are in sync, then you can slow your breath, soften your facial expressions, and lower your energy.

- When someone is yelling or talking loudly, you can match their vocal quality and then slowly lead them to lower their voice and change their tone.

While these tools may seem a bit more advanced for some, try them with a stranger, friend, or loved one (babies and kids love it). Practice makes perfect.

You are on your way to *acting* compassionately, which brings you one step closer to *being* compassionate.

Compassion In Action: Start by just noticing your behaviors when you are communicating with others. Are your arms crossed? Do you use eye-contact? As you become more aware of your own body, you can try on one or more of these rapport building tools.

Oh No! They're Crying, What Do I Do?

When my mom died in 2008, I somehow got the idea that I had to be strong for everyone else. At the funeral, my brother and I delivered the eulogy to more than a thousand people (which says a lot about how beloved my mom was in our community) and I didn't allow myself to cry. Not one single tear slipped out. I was so worried that if I wasn't this example of "strength," everyone else would fall apart. And since I didn't want that to happen, I assumed the role of the "strong" one.

Throughout life we are given tools for dealing with loss and change that don't particularly serve us. "Be strong" is a biggie, one that's ingrained in all of us. What happens if we aren't strong? What if we "fall apart"? What if we cry? What if we show real human emotion?

One lesson I have learned since then is that my "being strong" got in the way of my truth. When I pretended to be fine, I cut myself off from the very thing I needed the most at that time: other people's love and support during the hardest experience of my life. My inability to share how I was truly feeling was my source of disconnection. Hence, my "strength"—and I put strength in quotes because it is actually stronger to be vulnerable than it is to pretend to be fine—made me feel terribly alone.

Isn't it interesting how uncomfortable people seem to become when someone is crying? What is it about tears that evokes such discomfort? And what do most people say once someone starts crying? "Don't cry," "It's okay," or "I'm so sorry."

I want to tell you that you don't have to be sorry. In reality, crying is natural and provides quite a bit of healing. Think back to a time when you were upset and allowed yourself to cry. If you were in a safe place and gave in to the tears without being hushed or handed a tissue, how did you feel afterward?

In my experience, tears can act as a release, and being accepted and acknowledged during these moments has also been a powerful healing tool. I always tell my clients, "Tears are better out than in."

Next time someone begins to cry in your presence:

- Resist the urge to fix them.

- Stand or sit with them.

- Be present so they know crying is safe in your presence.

- Say, "It's okay to cry." (You can even say, "Tears are better out than in.")

- Try not to immediately run away to find a tissue or shush them (even if it is loving).

- After you have given them some time to be with their tears, you can ask if a hug would be helpful. If they accept, hug them but don't pat them; simply breathe with them.[16] If they say no to a hug, let that be okay.

You are not required to say anything, and sometimes it is more powerful if you don't. Silence and a hug can do wonders. If you feel comfortable saying something, acknowledge how they may be feeling by saying something like, "I can't imagine what you're going through, but thank you for sharing it with me."

If you think about it, it means a lot that someone is willing to cry in front of you. So be that safe space for them, and I promise you will be okay too. Crying is normal, healthy, and can be a powerful healing tool.

In an article by Judith Orloff, MD, author of the *New York Times* bestseller *Emotional Freedom: Liberate Yourself from Negative Emotions and Transform Your Life*, she explains that:

Emotional tears have special health benefits. Biochemist and "tear expert" Dr. William Frey at the Ramsey Medical Center in Minneapolis discovered that reflex tears are 98% water, whereas emotional tears also contain stress hormones which are excreted from the body through crying. After studying the composition of tears, Dr. Frey found that emotional tears shed these hormones and other toxins which accumulate during stress. Additional studies also suggest that crying

---

16   Grief Recovery Method Certification

stimulates the production of endorphins, our body's natural painkiller and "feel-good" hormones.

So go ahead, let the tears out, and allow the healing to begin!

One thing I am working on is my own vulnerability and comfort with crying or tearing up with people who care about me.

What about you? Can you allow yourself to feel? To cry?

Compassion In Action: How did you react the last time someone cried in front you? If you reacted compassionately, great, continue acting that way. If you were not as compassionate as you could have been, first, forgive yourself, then commit to acting more compassionately next time you are with someone who is crying. As an uplevel, you may want to reach out to the person, and if it feels appropriate you can apologize for not being more supportive.

PART IV: YOUR LIFE WITH COMPASSION

Chapter 15: Compassion Requires Selfishness

From the time we are young, we are taught to share, be generous, be thankful, and care about others. We're also taught that it's bad to be overly concerned with ourselves. If we care too much about our well-being, our desires, our hopes and dreams, we are considered selfish.

The very word has such a negative connotation that I would never want to be referred to as selfish. Why? Because it implies judgment. As I have mentioned, the trouble with judgment is that there is little to no compassion when we are judging. In other words, we don't see the positive intention in selfishness.

For centuries, we have valued martyrdom. The more we give, the better we are, even if it means that our own well-being goes by the wayside. We are so worried that we may seem selfish that we have almost gone too far in the other direction. In fact, using the word selfish to describe ourselves or others discourages us from receiving, and just as important, taking care of ourselves.

Compassionate Coaching Tip: Selfishness is not only a good thing, but it may be a key to healing our world.

That's right. You heard me. Being selfish, taking care of *you* first, is key to healing our world. Why? Because who benefits when you are taking care of yourself? When you feel good in your body, when you are exercising, eating well, doing personal growth work?

I can guarantee you that it isn't only you. Your family. Your friends. Your coworkers. Your kids. Your students. Your patients. Your clients. Everyone around you benefits.

I don't know about you, but when I feel good, I am nicer, more patient, more loving, and easier to be around. Could it be that being selfish—taking care of you first—can actually benefit everyone in your life?

Absolutely! When you feel good, they feel good. When I come home from working out, getting a massage, doing yoga, going for a walk, having lunch with a friend, or anything else that fills my cup, I have so much more to give to my husband, my daughter, and everyone else in my life.

We have been flying a lot lately, and because we have a young child, one of the flight attendants comes by each time and reminds us that if there is a change in cabin pressure, we need to put on our oxygen masks first before assisting the baby. But, oh no, isn't that *selfish*?

No! In the case of the oxygen mask, we would literally pass out if we didn't take care of ourselves first. And what good am I to my daughter if I am unconscious?

If being selfish still sounds bad, wrong, or uncomfortable, I want you to think of the last time you gave someone something. How good did it feel to give? Whether it was a compliment, a gift, a lift, or just a smile, didn't it fill you up to give to someone else? Of course! It feels amazing to give.

So, with that in mind, how can you deny someone else the opportunity to give? Does that mean you have to receive? Definitely, but in a good way. Be it a compliment, a gift, a lift, or a smile, learning how to receive, to say yes, and to say thank you is a gift to someone else.

Let's redefine the word selfish. Let's start to value taking care of ourselves, because when we give from a place of fullness or abundance, it is much more appealing for the recipient than giving from a place of emptiness or depletion.

Compassion In Action: Develop a self-care plan for yourself. List the 5-10 things that fill your cup when you are starting to feel stress, burn-out, or overwhelm. Next time you are feeling this way, practice using something from your list. You can even share this list with a close friend, coworker, or your partner. This way they can encourage you to use your self-care strategies.

Chapter 16: How to Avoid Carrying the Pain of the World

This chapter is for you if as a compassionate warrior, an undercover therapist, or a listening ear, you tend to take on other people's pain. Your ability to empathize, understand, and share the feelings of another is what makes you who you are. And I would never want to take that away. It is truly a gift.

However, what I do want is for you to be able to continue caring for people for the rest of your life without burning out, growing resentful, or neglecting your own self-care. So how do you go about being an empathetic person without feeling drained?

These first few strategies are preventative.

1. Acknowledge and validate. How is that better for the listener? Acknowledging and validating is better for the listener because it is actually a lot less work to validate than it is to come up with a solution. When you are listening with the mentality that you have to fix the person or give them a solution, you're not truly able to hear them. In your head, you're trying to come up with the best thing you can say to help them. While this is done with good intention, it can also lead to you offering them advice or a solution that they often aren't looking for.

Unless the person specifically says, "Please give me some advice," you are actually better off acknowledging and validating what they're going through. And from the standpoint of the listener, it's a lot less work and will help you avoid burnout. If you can be there for them without offering your opinion (unless they ask for it), you are less likely to become involved in the drama of the issue, which will prevent over-involvement.

2. Begin shifting your mentality about pain and hardship. When we understand pain as part of growth rather than something evil that happens, we can see someone on their growth journey in life. Seeing pain as part of growth takes away our need to fix the person who is struggling and allows them to be seen as whole, not broken. At the Grief Recovery Institute we say, "People are not broken; they are broken-hearted."

When we shift away from fixing, advice-giving, pitying, and judging, and instead begin validating the experience, we can stop carrying other people's hurt. Our curiosity can help us grow our compassion, but we don't have to carry the pain because we know it is part of their learning in this life. We can then focus less on giving advice and more on accepting their experiences as they are—heart to heart, rather than head to heart.

3. Set healthy boundaries. There are numerous books written on healthy boundaries, and I encourage you to read *Boundaries: When to Say Yes, When to Say No to Take Control of Your Life* by Dr. Henry Cloud and Dr. John Townsend. This book will give you great insight if you intuitively know that setting boundaries with others is challenging for you.

- For the moment, I want to share a few of the ways that I set boundaries. It starts with knowing yourself and knowing how you best interact with others, and then you express to others what you need.

For example, I don't love email, and I prefer in-person interactions. I also don't like urgency or feeling like I have to write people back immediately. So, I put up a full-time autoresponder on my email to let people know where I stand. It says something like, "Thanks for reaching out. I am busy being present in my life right now. I will respond in the next week, and please know that it isn't about you. Email is my least favorite way of communicating, but I will get back to you! If it is important, call me."

This may sound simple, but it has changed my life. I do the same thing on Facebook every six months or so. These examples are technological boundaries. However, it can be done in any part of your life where you feel like you are being drained.

As another example, do you have friends or colleagues who call, text, or email so often that you feel like you can't get anything done? Perhaps they have grown accustomed to your responding immediately. This is a difficult way to live. My recommendation, if you choose to accept it, is to tell these people that you are trying a new way of communicating. Let them know it isn't about them, but that you have found that you are addicted to your technology or that you are practicing taking breaks. Most people are supportive of these types of shifts, as long as you communicate that you are trying something different.

Don't be discouraged, however, if you are met with some resistance. If you do, stand by your request. I promise you, it will be better for everyone in the long run if you create and maintain healthy boundaries.

Finally, do you find yourself in conversations where the primary focus is complaining or speaking ill of someone else? If so, this may be an area in which you want to set some firm boundaries. You may be surprised, but these conversations can be energetically exhausting.

Here are a couple of ways to set boundaries:

1. Stop engaging in the negative conversation. Most people who gossip are looking for someone who will play along. If you stop participating, they will stop gossiping to you, preventing you from this type of energy drain.

2. Let people know your stand. This is a bit more confrontational, which may or may not be your style. If the first suggestion doesn't work, you can say something like, "I love chatting with you, and I don't mind if you need to vent (if that is true for you), but this month I'm on a bad-mouthing detox. So, if you don't mind, let's talk about something else."

Other Holistic Approaches for Releasing Pain and Preventing Burnout

This section is also known as *woo woo* or as new-age ways to cleanse your space and keep your energy pure. Ten years ago, I would have snubbed my nose at these methods. Energy was a foreign subject to me, and I would have asked, "What does that have to do with communication and connection?" and "How do they help prevent burnout?"

To some degree, we all know what energy is and sense it on a regular basis, some more than others.

Have you ever walked into a room and said, "Ugh, it sure is stuffy in here?" Or perhaps you were at a party or networking event and it felt ice cold? In neither of these cases am I talking about temperature. It can also work the other way; a room can feel warm and inviting as well. You can also feel when someone is upset. We don't always know why, but we can feel energetically that something is bothering them.

The first time I believed and experienced taking on someone else's energy was in late 2008 when I was in massage school. I'll preface this story by saying that we carry a lot of emotional energy in our gut, thus feeling sick to our stomach when we are upset.

As I was learning about abdominal massage that week in class and was required to give hours of massage outside of class for practice, I had scheduled a session for my brother the day before his LSAT (law school entrance exam) to help alleviate his stress before the exam. Not only was he stressed about the test, but he was also carrying the intense grief of our mom's death, less than a year earlier.

After the massage, where I practiced my new abdominal techniques, I became physically ill, yet he felt better. His sadness and anxious energy had transferred right over to me, and at that time I didn't have any tools to protect myself (partially because I didn't even believe in that concept).

Needless to say, I have never doubted energy transfer again, and I have since created rituals around protecting my energy and preventing burnout. I have also asked several other practitioners how they practice compassion and empathy without burning out.

Below you will find our techniques from the fairly basic to the extremely spiritual. If it feels weird or bizarre, that's okay. New things often do. If it works, do it. If it makes you feel better, do it. If it doesn't, try something else.

Remember, a lot of these suggestions are about setting clear intentions with your boundaries. If your intention is clear, you are more likely going to be able to hold a firm boundary. Remember, the more you are able to care for yourself, the more likely you will be able to help others.

1) Have a safe and confidential person you can vent to.

2) Breathe. Take deep cleansing breaths, inhaling positive energy and exhaling negative, toxic energy.

3) Wash your hands. I recommend thirty seconds all the way up to the elbows, and I would even include some deep breaths.

4) Shower. Water can be very cleansing. Even if you simpy stand there and let the water flow over your body, it can be a nice way to cleanse and release any negativity you have encountered.

5) Take an Epsom salt bath. Hot water works like a charm. You can even throw in some lavender or eucalyptus essential oil. You might also light a candle for calming energy.

6) Change your clothes. Sometimes switching outfits can be just what you need to let go of anything you took on from someone else.

7) Remove yourself from the space. You may need a change of scenery, so if you remove yourself with the intention of leaving behind whatever you just took on, it can leave you feeling cleansed and rejuvenated.

8) Take a walk or do some movement. Walking or exercise of any kind can help to release toxins and negative energy, while boosting endorphins and helping you generate more positive energy in your body.

9) Journal. I love to write—whatever is bothering me, I simply rant and get it all out. Once I am finished, I tear it up and throw it away.

10) Bring your wrists together at the solar plexus (just underneath your chest) and let your hands rest on your arms. As you do so, take several cleansing breaths, allowing any negative energy to move through and away from you.

11) Practice meditation. Find a mantra, saying, or sound that soothes you. You can start with something like, "We are all perfect

the way we are." Sit quietly for a few minutes with your eyes closed, focused on your breath. If this seems interesting to you, look into taking a meditation or mindfulness class. I began a meditation course and daily practice with Kelvin Chin from TurningWithin.org.

12) Clean your space. You can eliminate clutter by sweeping, mopping, or dusting, or you can organize the area in such a way that your physical space is representing how you want your internal space to feel—clear!

13) Practice visualization. Before you go into a session, or as you begin connecting with someone about something emotionally taxing, close your eyes. Visualize a little bubble barrier around your body with glowing yellow, healing light. Set the intention that nothing comes in or goes out of this healing bubble, but that both people will benefit from its glow.

14) Cleanse with smudging. The Native American practice of smudging, or purifying a room with the smoke of sacred herbs, can help clear negative energy from a space. And the apparent benefits are steeped in science: when burned, sage and other herbs release negative ions, which research has linked to a more positive mood. For more information on the practice of smudging, check out Diane Ronngren's book *Sage and Smudge: The Ultimate Guide*.

15) Open up your space. Open all windows and curtains to let fresh air and sunlight in. This is an easy way to cleanse a house or a room's energy.

16) Spray your space with saltwater or rose water spray. Both types help cleanse the physical space where you are or where you have been working with someone. I like to spray it in the corners and all around where we have been.

The thing about being a caregiver or a listening ear is that you have to take care of yourself or you will burn out. Remember, caring for you is *not* a selfish act. It is a way to ensure longevity in your career or life as a caring person.

Chapter 17: How to Have Compassion for Yourself During Painful Transitions

As I peered across the playground, I noticed a woman and her son sitting on a bench by the swings. Admiring their interaction and her adorable child, our eyes met and we exchanged a smile. Half an hour later, she and her son came running back frantically in search of something. Curiously, I asked if there was something I could help her find. She said, "I lost my cell phone and can't remember where all we've been."

I picked up my daughter and we walked over to the bench where they had been sitting. Sure enough, it was right there. She thanked me profusely and proceeded to share how chaotic her life was—she and her family had moved four times in the last year, and she felt like she didn't know which way was up.

With my background in grief, I reassured her how natural it is to feel discombobulated when things are changing in your life. I shared the definition of grief—"the conflicting feelings that come at the end of or change in a familiar pattern of behavior"—and how the best thing she could do in this moment was to be kind and patient with herself and her family. She hugged and thanked me, then slowly walked away with a little more self-compassion.

No matter the transition, be it a move, a career change, a milestone, or a loss, it can be challenging to take a step back, realize that what you are experiencing is normal, and show yourself a little compassion.

Here are several tools that my clients and I have found helpful during our transitions.

- Acknowledge that your experience is okay just as it is. If you are having a hard time, an easy time, or mixed reviews . . . it is okay. Whatever you are experiencing is fine because it is unique to you. Everyone, including ourselves, wants us to be happy, but that simply isn't always the case. Sometimes being uncomfortable or unhappy can help guide us to what is more "right" for us.

- Listen inward instead of outward. During a transition, I encourage you to determine your values. What is most important to you? As I remind myself, my husband, and my clients, "You are the only person who has to go to bed and wake up with your decision every day. If it is only for someone else, then it probably isn't the right decision for you." Don't allow outside influences to sway you. Instead, take some time to get clear about what you need and let those feelings guide you.

- Take care of yourself. What are some things you can do for yourself regularly that make you feel good? Is it movement, eating well, spending time in nature, journaling, socializing, sleeping, receiving a massage, etc.? Whatever it is, do a little something for yourself every day. It can be as small as taking a shower and giving yourself a couple extra minutes of downtime.

- Have honest, open communication. Ask for what you want and don't want. There are nice ways of setting boundaries. People can't read your mind, so if you set them up for success by telling them how you feel and what you need, you are more likely going to be engaged in a situation that works for both of you.

- Remember that these feelings are temporary. My grandmother and mother loved to use the expression, "This too shall pass." It is true for both positive and negative experiences. When I am feeling down, I remind myself that this too shall pass. When I am feeling good, I remember that this too shall pass. This gives me perspective on my current experience and a greater appreciation for life.

Whatever you are going through right now, be gentle with yourself.

As Maya Angelou said, "When you know better, you do better."

Listen inward and the truth will become clear.

Chapter 18: How to Practice Compassion When You Are in the Trenches of Life

Have you ever looked in the mirror and not liked what you saw? Sometimes when I feel ugly or fat, I am not as nice to others because I am not being kind to myself.

And guess what? Not being kind to yourself can go much deeper than the surface. When you are going through a breakup, a divorce, a lawsuit, a job change, or the death of someone you love, it can be challenging to show up for others as our best, most compassionate self, because we feel awful about ourselves.

Here is how to be compassionate toward others when you are in your darkest moments:

- Remember, it is your humanity that makes you a compassionate friend, confidant, and caregiver. Know that the experiences you have been through are helping give you compassion for your clients, family, and friends. While you may be in pain right now, this experience is part of your growth and compassion education. The more life experience you have, the more you are able to help others.

- Be compassionate toward yourself the way you would be toward the people in your life. Your perfection isn't what makes you a good friend. It is your ability to walk by someone's side, to listen deeply, and to accept them where they are. Self-compassion means relating kindly to yourself. Acknowledging your own story and honoring your grief journey are part of that, so don't diminish what you are going through.

- Even caregivers need help. Seek support from family, friends, or a professional. As renowned shame and vulnerability researcher Dr. Brené Brown says, "Vulnerability sounds like truth and feels like courage. Truth and courage aren't always comfortable, but they're never weakness." This vulnerability is what brings us together. By sharing with others what you are going through, you will likely be able to connect more deeply and feel less alone.

Make a list of people or activities that you enjoy and that don't diminish your energy. Reach out and ask for a coffee date, a movie, or a phone visit. Tell them what you need by asking, "Do you mind if I tell you what's going on with me?"

- Know when you need to reschedule or take the day off. There are days and moments where you definitely need to take some time for you (without guilt). Perhaps you can't get out of bed— emotionally or physically. If so, it is okay to reschedule with a friend in need or take a personal day. You have to take care of yourself first. As compassionate warriors, we have to give from abundance rather than depletion. When we are depleted by our own life experiences, it is even more important to fill ourselves up first.

- Know that you are not alone. You are not a superhero and you don't have to be. When I am leading a course, teaching a class, or coaching someone and I tear up, people always share that they are grateful that I'm not perfect either.

It is our humanity that makes us compassionate, not our perfection.

So, if you are going through your own stuff, take care of yourself, be kind to yourself, seek support, enjoy people or activities that fill you up, or reschedule. Know that it is all part of the journey, and you are doing it beautifully.

Compassionate Coaching Tip: Visualize your perfect day from the moment you wake up until the time you go to bed. What are you doing? What are you wearing? Who do you hang out with? What do you eat? How do you smell? What do you see? How do you feel? Now, while this day may not be 100% possible, find something in that day that you can act on now. Perfect days don't usually create themselves: sometimes we have to orchestrate them.

Chapter 19: When Compassion Feels Really Hard

"True compassion recognizes that all the boundaries we perceive between ourselves and others are an illusion." —Madisyn Taylor

In the HBO series *Game of Thrones*, there is a scene where a religious extremist is talking to the queen. She asks him why she has a hard time loving the homeless and the impoverished. He profoundly responds that seeing people who are struggling, who are stripped of possessions, beautiful clothing, and nice smells, are a reminder of the shadow side of ourselves. They are a reminder of our deepest fears of who we would be without our masks. They remind us of our human imperfections.

> **Compassionate Coaching Tip:** Consider that the people with whom we have the hardest time being compassionate are the people who most represent the parts of ourselves we haven't accepted. In other words, if you are having a hard time having compassion for someone, consider that they most represent a part of you that you're not ready to accept.

With that in mind, what is it about others that most annoys you? Generally speaking, it is a quality in ourselves that we fear having. If you are bossy, you may become annoyed by bossy people. If you talk a lot, you may be easily annoyed by chatterboxes.

I've noticed that I don't like when people are positive to the point of seeming insincere, and yet I have spent a lot of time exuding positivity myself, even at times when I don't feel good. I tend to be critical of people who are vain, but the truth is that vanity is a part of myself I don't like. I don't want to be vain, but I know I can be. I want to love myself exactly as I am *au naturel*. Sometimes I do, but I also know that I like to look and feel beautiful.

If you are having a hard time being patient or compassionate toward someone else, ask yourself:

1) If I am completely honest with myself, is this a quality that I, too, possess? If so, how can I accept that part of myself?

2) What can I learn from this person? If I am annoyed, perhaps I am supposed to learn patience. If I am angry, perhaps I am supposed to learn compassion.

The following exercise is an adaptation from the Transformational Coaching Method to help shift judgment to love. It is best to start with the self.

Exercise: Shifting Judgment to Love[17]

What would you like? (e.g., to thrive in my life, to feel more at peace with a loved one's death, to lose the weight I gained since my grandma died, to be more compassionate, etc.)

---

17 Derived from the Transformational Coaching Method

What will having that do for you? (e.g., achieve love, safety, belonging, happiness, etc.)

How will you know when you have it? What will you see, hear, and feel? (e.g., I'll be smiling more, I'll be fifteen pounds lighter, I'll spend more time with friends, etc.)

How do you feel right now? (e.g., I don't feel like exercising. I don't like spending time with my friends. I'm too exhausted to do anything, etc.)

Let's make a list of all the judgments you have about yourself. Include all the things you tell yourself you *should* do, but that you *don't* do. Say the judgments aloud as if you are talking to yourself. (e.g., "You don't exercise enough." "You should be over this by now." "You push your friends away," etc.)

What if this weren't true? (e.g., What if you already exercised the perfect amount? How do you know you are alienating your friends?)

Now that we have looked at some of your judgments, do you know what the cure is for judgment?

The cure for judgment is curiosity, so I'm going to ask you to become really curious. We're going to walk through a simple process that helps trade in judgment for curiosity so we can see ourselves in a new light.

The judgment you'd like to shift is (choose the most painful judgment from above):

Underneath judgment is usually some degree of anger and fear, which tends to carry an underlying message for us that we may not always see on the surface. Let's see what we can discover there.

The first step is ANGER. Fill in the blank: "I am angry with myself for _____."

(e.g., letting my job get in the way of my relationship)

The second step is FEAR. Fill in the blank: "If I don't change, I'm afraid I will _____."

(e.g., never get married and have children)

The third step is a REQUEST. Fill in the blank: "This judgment has done a great job of _____ (positive intention—keeping me feeling loved, safe, happy, or part of something), and I want to let go of (this judgment) _____

so that I can _____."

The fourth step is LOVE. Repeat after me: "I love myself!" (Just try it)

I deserve (to be happy, to find love, to have a balanced life, etc.)

I want to feel (supported, joyful, loved, safe, etc.) _____

Good. Thank you for that. Now picture yourself one year from now being exactly where you want to be. What do you have? (paint a picture of yourself where you want to be)

Now, close your eyes and step into that version of you.

Imagine that it's one year from now, having already achieved everything you wanted, and I run into you on the street. I ask, "How are things?" In response, imagine telling me about how that one exercise you did last year was a huge turning point.

I then say, "Wow! I'm so happy for you. What choices did you make back then that set you up for success? Were there any obstacles you had to overcome? What did you have to let go of in order to get to the next stage of your evolution?" Fill those in below.

Now let's move to the next segment . . .

Have you ever loved someone? A family member, a friend, a child, a partner? Good. Think of someone you love tremendously—someone who makes you feel joyful when you see or think of them. (they can be living or dead).

Good. What is his/her name? Close your eyes and picture that person. Imagine the smile on his/her face when you appear. Feel how much you love them and how much they love you too. Do you feel that?

Excellent. So there you are, one year from now, having everything you want and feeling full of love. Taking that wisdom that got you here and all the love you have, notice that you have an urge to turn and see yourself a year ago. As you make eye contact with that version of you, send him/her all the love you feel. Shower him/her with this love and reassure him/her that he/she made it.

Finally, tell him/her anything that would be useful to know to say YES and take empowered action so that this journey is the most pleasurable one.

Great work! How does that feel?

Hopefully you now see that compassion and judgment cannot coexist. Whenever you are having a hard time shifting from judgment to compassion, come back to this exercise, work on another judgment, and start finding compassion for yourself.

Compassion and Anger

Our first inclination when faced with challenging situations or rude people is usually to become mad or sad. Anger is part of our fight or flight response, and it is natural to feel anger or frustration when things don't go our way or when we feel threatened. It is part of our survival; however, in modern times, it is typically not the case that we are in physical danger, so we have to retrain ourselves to think and then feel with compassion rather than our first instinct, which is anger.

Think about a time when someone did or said something to you that threatened your belief. Perhaps they made fun of you or said something mean about someone you care about. I know that my first instinct is to be mad, to think negative thoughts, or even have a name-calling session in my head.

Similar to overeating, getting drunk, or using any numbing behavior that isn't good for us when used in excess, blaming and anger can feel good in the moment, but they don't feel good in the long run. They are not healthy for our well-being, and they can cause long-term damage. Reacting with anger can feel good in that second, but afterward we are often left feeling sad, alone, ashamed, and wishing we had done it differently.

My mom used to say, "Never say anything in anger because you can't ever take it back." I extend that to shared writing as well. Saying or writing unkind things typically leads to regret. If you are feeling frustrated or upset and need to get it out, I would recommend writing it down. Spill your feelings on paper, however you see fit (I prefer stream-of-consciousness writing) and then get rid of it. Tear it up, burn it (safely of course), shred it. Whatever you choose is fine, but dispose of it. As you rip it up, shred it, or burn it, take a deep breath in and then out . . . and let go of the pain and negative thoughts. If there are more, you have more writing to do. Then repeat the "getting rid of" part.

If you have something you want to say or write to the person with whom you feel angry, do it after this exercise. You will be able to write with a clearer head. If you write something that you want to give to that person, hold onto it for three to five days. Once the allotted time has passed, read the letter again and check in with yourself. Ask, "Do I still want to send this? Will this do more good than harm? Does this still represent how I feel?"

This method helps to deal with anger or frustration when what you truly want to feel is compassion.

Another way is to vent to someone safe.

Characteristics of someone safe:

- will acknowledge what you are feeling rather than diminish it

- won't judge you or hold whatever you are saying over your head later

- won't encourage you to feel angrier than you already do

- will keep your thoughts and feelings confidential

As we examine the immediate response when faced with antagonistic situations, anger, or sadness, it brings up another important point: compassion is something we can think about, but it is best used in conjunction with our hearts. We can justify why we need compassion, but ultimately, we must move from the head into the heart.

In order to drop into our hearts, we must remind ourselves that it likely has nothing to do with us, that the person has a story that we don't know, and that more healing is done by offering compassion and understanding than anger.

Compassion In Action: Is there a person or recurring situation in your life where it is currently difficult for you to practice compassion? You may to script out or practice how you will respond compassionately the next time you face this person or situation. What tools will you use to respond more compassionately in the moment?

Check out the section about feeling compassion for people with different beliefs on pg. 153 for more insight.

Compassion for Teens and Young People

Middle school and high school can be brutal. Kids are mean, partially because it is a confusing time and partially because their hormones are raging. Because they are experiencing so many changes, they don't always know how to communicate or have a safe person to communicate with who won't judge them or tell them not to feel bad.

Now that you have learned the myths of grief from the Grief Recovery Institute, you can better understand why there are so few safe places to turn when we are feeling our feelings. Most adults will say something like:

"You think this is hard? Being an adult is harder."

"Oh, don't feel bad about your girlfriend breaking up with you. That was just puppy love."

The unfortunate thing is that these feelings are the most intense these young people have ever felt.

Another example is college. I remember how scared and excited I was about going to college, yet my scared part was met with, "You're about to be in college. That's the best time of your life!" This phrase diminished all the change going on in me. With so much emphasis about how great it should be, and will be, young people often end up feeling this weird guilt and isolation if they feel bad. *What's wrong with me?* is often the first thing we think when we imagine we are "supposed" to be happy but we aren't.

No matter our age, when our expectations aren't aligned with our reality, it can create pain and personal criticism. This disconnect between our reality and our expectations of reality is where self-compassion must be born. We must relate kindly to ourselves so we can relate kindlier to others.

When I find myself in self-criticism, asking myself if I am enough, I return to this concept of loving myself.

I am enough as I am.

When I honor my pain, my compassion grows. The pains of life give our Compassion Hat new feathers or jewels. Thus, all the painful experiences I've felt give me more compassion for others. While I dread having to go through it in the moment, I am grateful for the losses of my life and even the pain, because they allow me to relate more deeply with others.

Garth Brooks sings in his famous song, "The Dance" about being glad he did not know how everything would work out. That if he'd known about the pain, if he'd missed it, he would have also missed the dance. In other words, while the pain is hard, it's a part of the richness of life.

So if you have a teen in your life who is going through a tough time, how can you practice more compassion for them? Try some of the tools outlined in this book. It may be as simple as listening without offering solutions, or even sharing how there was a time when you were in high school where you, too, felt devastated, heartbroken, disappointed, or lost.

Teens' hormones are often impacting how they are feeling, and everything can feel quite intense. Let them know that they are not alone, that this is normal, and that it won't always be this way.

This is a time where your teen needs you. According to parenting experts, teenagers and toddlers require the most emotional support from their parents or caregivers, as they are highly confusing times where they are figuring out themselves and their boundaries. If you are beating yourself up about how you relate to your teen, it is a great opportunity to try on your Compassion Hat, for both yourself and him/her. Remember, you didn't know what you didn't know, and now you do.

Compassion In Action: It is easy to think teens are being dramatic. Try to remember what it was like back then. Check in with them to see how they are doing and try to acknowledge rather than fix. For example, instead of saying, "Don't worry, Stephanie won't be your friend in a couple years when you go to college anyway." You can try saying, "Is it hard that you and Stephanie aren't getting along? You girls have been friends for a long time."

Why Celebrities Need Compassion Too

Many of us forget, but celebrities are people too. Can you imagine being constantly judged, analyzed, and criticized for everything you do? I can't.

It is easy to justify being critical of celebrities by saying things like, "They have it all," or "They're asking for it." But are they? Sometimes, people are simply good at their craft. Sometimes, people are following their hearts. Sometimes they are famous before they are even adults making their own decisions.

They, like us, are people who experience losses, but unfortunately for them it is often under the microscope of the public eye. The tabloids exploit any moment they don't look "their best," any relationship drama, or addiction problem. Those things are difficult when you are under the radar, so I can't imagine what it is like to be blatantly criticized merely because you are famous.

Does fame have to be associated with exposure to more hatred?

Some people say that celebrities are lucky because they receive special treatment. I want to point out that they also receive especially poor treatment a lot of the time. Look at some of the people who have been deeply impacted by their fame in modern-day media:

Michael Jackson. "What a pervert," you say? Who would you be if you could never leave your house without swarms of people swooning around you? What would it be like to not know who your friends are or to have parents who abused you? What would it be like to always wish you were someone else?

Now, I am not saying that I condone any of the things that Michael Jackson did or was accused of doing, but I do believe in being compassionate so that we can prevent future hurt.

Amy Winehouse. A British singer, songwriter who truly had it all, until she didn't. If you haven't seen the documentary about her life, I highly recommend it. It is a great perspective of how it is to live as a celebrity when you didn't want to be famous. This young woman had a gift, and she loved to express herself. However, her fame and the public eye became a magnifying glass for her unresolved grief. People were utterly terrible to her when she was in a dark place because we tend to discount famous people's heartache.

Justin Bieber and Miley Cyrus are two others who became famous quite young. We are highly critical of their behavior, but we have to remember that they are simply trying to figure it out like everyone else. I can't imagine never having any privacy. Yes, they have fame and fortune, but that isn't always the easiest life, and it certainly doesn't make a person immune to heartache.

My hope is that you begin to see that celebrities are people too. A friend recently told me that she had given up reading celebrity magazines, after she herself had gone through a difficult divorce. She realized that she was using these celebrity stories to escape her own life. Now she says she lives her own version of life that has much more star quality to it. She moved to a new city, spends more quality time with friends she loves, and has even started dating again. The drama that she was so addicted to in those magazines isn't nearly as exciting as her own life.

As a side note, celebrities don't just live in Hollywood. I highlighted some extreme examples above, but celebrities can also be people in our lives who we think "have it all" or "deserve whatever happens"— meaning our own local celebrities, including the popular kids in school or the lady at work who seems to receive all the accolades.

Compassion In Action: Perhaps we can spend less time focused on what is wrong with celebrities (A-list or local) and more time focusing on what we can do to continue improving our own lives. If you go back to the idea of replacing the word jealous with the word inspire, how can you make the most of your life?

How to Have Compassion for People with Different Beliefs

Sometimes I find myself feeling frustrated or even angry with people I consider close-minded, rude, racist, sexist, or any other prejudice. My belief is that it is important to be kind to all people. I identify with this belief and therefore consider myself a good person.

The funny thing about this idea is that by judging others for their closed-off beliefs, I am in fact being close-minded myself.

Prejudice against prejudice is still prejudice.

I think we all forget sometimes that we don't have to agree with others all the time, and just because someone has these beliefs doesn't mean I have to identify with them. What I try to do is understand that their beliefs are something they hold dear and that my judging them isn't going to change that.

Do you know that more than 70% of our beliefs are formed by the time we are only five years old? Knowing this helps feed our compassion because we start to realize that our beliefs come from things we learned when we were likely quite young. It doesn't mean we have to condone the belief or agree with it, but we can be compassionate toward people for more peace of mind and less conflict.

So, what is a belief?

According to the *Etymology Dictionary*, "belief" comes from the West Germanic *ga-laubon,* which means "to hold dear; esteem; or trust." When we seek to have a compassionate response to people with differing beliefs, it can help us understand where they are coming from and how they arrived at their current belief system.

Our beliefs help us make sense of the world, and we hold on tightly to our beliefs because the world can be confusing, and because new or different thoughts can be intimidating. When we are struggling through a loss or a challenging transition, we lean back on our belief system to help us find our way. We are constantly looking for evidence that our beliefs are true because it helps us navigate the world and justify our feelings and actions.

When we are in conversation with someone who has a different belief, if we want to be compassionate, we can shift from reacting to responding. And as Jon Mertz, thought leader and author of *Activate Leadership: Aspen Truths to Empower Millennial Leaders* puts it, the difference between reacting and responding is mindfulness. And for our purposes, being mindful means stepping back from the conversation, taking a deep breath, putting on our Compassion Hat, and bringing reason to the table alongside emotion.

Reactions can seem defensive, and as Mertz shares, "There is a downside to reacting. We let emotions without reason drive us forward. We lose control. Reacting is sporadic and emotional."

However, when we step back, take a breath, and put on our Compassion Hat, we can respond more effectively. And the "upside of a solid response," as Mertz reminds us, "is an engaging conversation, all positive and all civil. We learn. We grow. We listen. We respond. We act forthrightly and from within."[18]

Another basic tool for shifting beliefs within ourselves or staying open to other people's beliefs is acknowledgement of the positive intention of the belief. You want to ask, "How is this belief serving me?" Or, "How is their belief serving them?"

---

18   https://www.thindifference.com/2013/03/a-mindful-difference-respond-vs-react/

Compassionate Coaching Tip: Another tip for trying to understand someone's belief is by responding with the thought: *Is this an act of love or a cry for love?*[19]

When people say or do hurtful things that are critical of our beliefs, it is to our benefit to not take it personally. For example, every now and again, I will receive a hateful email. One I got recently told me that they were disappointed in me for preying on vulnerable people.

My first reaction was defensive: "How dare they say that about me!" Then I took a step back, took a breath, and put on my Compassion Hat. I asked myself, "Is this an act of love or a cry for love?" It was clear that it was a cry for love.

My compassionate response was to acknowledge that this person was probably hurting, which is most likely why she wrote such a judgmental email to me. When I didn't take it personally, it allowed me to respond to her thoughtfully, graciously, and nonviolently. I also felt better about the interaction because I didn't make what she said mean anything about me.

Love wins. Every time.

---

19   Transformational Coaching Method

Compassion In Action: As a kid I went to church with friends, and as an adult I participate in other people's religious and cultural customs. It gives me a chance to try on someone else's belief system with curiosity. Do you have a friend who has a different faith tradition, culture, or background than you? If so, ask if you can participate in a special gathering or holiday next time it happens. Be respectful, ask questions with curiosity, and learn.

Why and How to Have Compassion for a Killer (or someone accused of a horrible crime)

Since September 11th, we have seen an increasing number of national tragedies. More mass shootings, more hate crimes, more violence—a world divided. We see it everywhere, and the world is feeling less safe.

Every day, I avoid watching the news because I know what I will see. I don't want to see it because it breaks my heart, but just like I say with grief, the more we avoid our feelings the louder they become. The more I pretend this hatred and violence doesn't exist, the louder it gets. I can continue to live in my bubble, but the truth is, people are hurting.

I deal with the aftermath of people's pain daily. But I am also realizing more and more that I need to be involved in the prevention of pain. I know that life is hard and that challenging things will happen; people will die, heartache will come, and I am grateful to have tools for that, both for myself and others.

However, I also have tools in the form of compassion, validation, understanding, acceptance, and love. These tools are all at the heart of changing the world for the better.

It is easy to live and think in black and white, but the gray is where the change happens. The gray is where we try to see the other side. The gray is where we put our Compassion Hat and Grief-Colored Glasses on. It is where we look at the pain and suffering of individuals and recognize that everyone has a story behind their actions, behind their façade of "I'm fine."

When I hear about a murderer, my first thought is, *What must have happened to him or her?*

I want to make something clear: I do not condone the behavior. And I do not agree with the actions. Rather, I am trying to understand the gray by asking the question, "What pain, what loss, what heartache is that person carrying around that led to such explosive behavior?"

There's a saying that goes something like, "I'm not doing _____ because I want to. I'm doing it because I don't know how else to cope with the pain." By thinking about any addiction or extreme behavior in this way, you can build compassion for people who use coping tools that you can't understand.

I recognize exaggerated cases exist where people have extreme mental illness or ideology, and I also know that most people who do horrendous things are people who are merely hurting. Unfortunately, their inner hurt reaches a breaking point where they lash out at others or hurt themselves. These outward explosions can range from anger to road rage, physical abuse to murder, and mass shootings to war. All of these are unacceptable behaviors.

You may be wondering how and why you should be compassionate toward these people.

Let's start with the why.

Curiosity and compassion for people who do horrible things is the only way to prevent future hate. Compassion is the key to healing a world full of pain and hatred. If we hate someone who does something terrible, we are continuing the cycle and doing exactly what we don't want—creating more hate and more fear. We are also causing self-harm by harboring such anger and rage ourselves.

As I mentioned early in the book, "Resentment is the poison we take in hopes that someone else dies." When we refuse to put on our Compassion Hat and hold onto resentment, we hold onto our own pain, potentially becoming what we resent or don't understand.

Now for the how.

How can you find it in your heart to have compassion for someone who has hurt others?

I start superficially by asking the question, "What must they be going through that led to this action?" Then I go a little deeper and ask, "What has happened to them in their lifetime that led to such pain and hurt that they have this explosive behavior toward others?

Then I go to the next level where I imagine them as a small baby. I think of the challenges they may have faced, and the hurt they must have had. I think of how they didn't receive the love they needed or experienced a tremendous amount of grief. I wonder what hopes and dreams they had that did not come to fruition.

Then I go the opposite way. If they are still alive, I think, *How will their actions affect them? What will their journey be like moving forward?*

As I shared earlier, my mom was crossing the street and was run over by a young man in a pickup truck. This total freak accident changed my life and the lives of hundreds and even thousands of others. I know that accidental killing is different than intentional killing, but I want to share a short story about my personal experience.

While I do not condone what happened, I do feel compassion for the young man who ran over my mom. I feel sad that he has to live with the fact that he killed someone's mother, someone's wife, someone's friend, someone's mentor, someone's teacher, someone's daughter, someone's sister—every single day for the rest of his life. I don't know what he's done with this pain, sadness, or guilt, but I do feel for him. I hope with all my heart that he doesn't hurt himself or anyone else because of the weight he carries around from having killed my mom.

Some may think I'm crazy that I don't hold a grudge or that I'm not angry, but I know my anger would only hurt me. And I am sad enough. Hating him or being angry with him would only feed a cycle that I don't want to see in this world—the perpetration of more hatred and more anger. Rather, I want to create a world with more love, more understanding, more compassion, and more people trying to live in the gray. I also know that my mom, while perfectly capable of holding a grudge on my behalf when she was alive, would not want me to live my life hating this young man either.

I hope that you do not take my words and my hope for a compassionate and loving society as a dismissal or a diminishing of the horrific murders, hate crimes, bigotry, hatred, racism, sexism, homophobia, and other forms of intolerance and violence that are going on in our world. They are not.

I do not dismiss or diminish the pain that has been caused by terrible acts and words; my heart aches for the victims of these tragedies. My message to you is to not create more hate.

As someone once said to me, "Hurt people hurt people."

The thought of someone killing my daughter brings tears to my eyes, and the thought that so many sons and daughters, brothers and sisters, friends and lovers, have been killed in unthinkable acts of violence causes me to shake my head and wonder what kind of world we are living in.

My challenge to you in these circumstances is to look curiously at a killer and think about what must have happened in their life for them to get to the place where they could do such a terrible thing.

Compassion starts from understanding that people are hurting, and if not given the right tools or the right outlet, they will hurt themselves or others in ways that break our hearts.

My love, my hope, and my compassion goes out to the family and friends and all of those who are devastated by the many tragedies of life.

Bring love to the world. Love the people around you. Be compassionate for those you don't understand and don't put people into a box. My fear is that there will continue to be more hatred for people we don't understand or who have different beliefs than we do, creating an ever-expanding world of hatred and misunderstanding.

I know sometimes it takes magic or a miracle, but please put on your Grief-Colored Glasses, put on your Compassion Hat, and look at the world with compassion and curiosity, asking, "What is the story behind this person's actions?"

End hate. Embrace love and compassion.

Chapter 20: Now What?

Now that you have received a toolkit of practical and philosophical ways to be compassionate, the next step is to convert this new knowledge to wisdom. Knowledge turns to wisdom through experience, and we gain experience by practicing.

Two key elements to being a compassionate listener are presence and connection. My hope is that you take your favorite philosophies and new communication skills and use them regularly. See what works for you. Notice how people respond.

Taking the Next Step with Compassion

Part of continuing your compassion training is to recognize that self-compassion is key. You have to continue exploring your own stories, honoring your losses, and celebrating your joys. Having a better understanding of yourself and your life will allow you to continue growing your compassion for others.

If you want to learn about supporting people through their most challenging grief experiences, check out The Grief Recovery Method Certification. Whether you want to participate as a griever or simply learn as a means to help others, you will be grateful for the toolkit you receive. And if you want to learn how to think, speak, act, and be compassionate, please visit www.laurajack.com to learn more about The Compassion Code Basic Training.

Are You the One with the Broken Heart?

David R. Cope, author of *The Rule Book of Life*, shares:

As a culture, we are unconsciously taught not to feel, for feelings expose parts of ourselves we compulsively hide—our dark side—that if revealed would be our certain demise. Yet, if we as a culture were taught the opposite, that feelings were just an opportunity for self-discovery, we could transcend pain, unhappiness, disease, and malaise. For the root of suffering is not life but our incapacity to feel. Feeling is freedom: freedom from the burdens of not feeling—life unbridled.

So many times in life, we are looking at everyone else and seeing their pain. But we are afraid to honestly look at our own feelings and experiences with a compassionate heart. Here are a few more tips to heal your heart.

1) Sometimes people say things that are hurtful, especially when we are hurting. Let it go. If we hold onto resentment against someone for what they don't know, it only hurts us more. Finding peace is a choice we make for ourselves. Recognize that they haven't been taught what to say or how to act, and feel free to give them this book.

2) People can't read our minds. Set up the people in your life for success by telling them what you need. Hopefully, through this book, you are tapping more into your truth and will therefore be able to ask for what you need more easily. For example, after my mom died, my husband Aaron would say, "Don't cry." Finally, I told him, "Please just tell me it's okay to cry . . . and then just hold me until I ask you to stop." Years later, he is still the best support when I am struggling.

3) Take baby steps each day to rediscover yourself. Let it be an adventure worth waking up for. You are the ONLY person you will always have in your life for certain.

4) Utilize the resources in the next section and be willing to try anything with a beginner's mind.

Here is the layout of a program I created to rediscover your light after loss. First are the foundational principles of the program, followed by the key elements to begin thriving in your life after any loss.

Take a little time to internalize these paradigms. Which ones resonate with you the most?

- The only way out is through. In other words, we have to feel to heal. We must embrace all emotion, including pain, to begin our journey to thriving.

- When we experience loss of any kind, it is normal to feel a mixture of emotions. There is nothing wrong with you if you are sad, relieved, angry, frustrated, scared, or any other emotion.

- Acknowledging our loss and experiencing our grief can increase the likelihood of growth.

- Comparing leads to despairing. No one wins when we judge other people's losses or our own. Your loss is important to you, and that is that.

- Thriving doesn't mean you will never feel sad again. It means that you can live your life fully and experience the full range of human emotion, including joy, sorrow, and everything in between.

- Thriving also means you have a choice about how you respond to the circumstances of your life rather than being a victim of your experience. We must acknowledge where we are honestly, what we have experienced, and what we have learned in order to begin the shift from surviving to thriving.

- Time does not heal our emotional wounds if we don't take action to care for them.

- Just as the ground after a fire is the most fertile place for growth, our life after loss has the potential for a new beginning we never thought possible.

- Our challenges have the opportunity to be the greatest learning lessons of our lives, which we then get to share with the world.

- Taking care of yourself is not selfish; it is actually key to thriving.

ABCs of Surviving to Thriving

Acknowledge

The first step of the program is to acknowledge where you are—not where you were or where you will be, but where you are right now.

It is also important to understand the difference between surviving and thriving as we begin this journey. Surviving means "to continue to live or exist, especially in spite of danger or hardship." Thriving means "to grow or develop well; prosper; flourish."

Before we make this shift, we must first acknowledge that we are surviving. I also invite you to acknowledge that your reaction to your circumstances, your loss, and your pain is normal and natural. Surviving—or barely getting by—is not bad or wrong. It is perfectly appropriate ... until it isn't. And the only person who can decide that is YOU.

The fact that you are here means that you are ready to make the shift to thriving. Not to worry ... we will take it one baby step at a time.

The first thing we can do to acknowledge our experience is to reflect upon our story. When we understand our own story and honor what we have been through without diminishing it, we pave the way for compassion toward ourselves and then others.

Compassion In Action:
- Write as much as you can about the loss and subsequent transition that brought you here. Do your best not to judge yourself.
- Draw a picture and illustrate your story. Don't worry about whether you think it's a "good" drawing or not. This is about letting everything out.
- If a song could represent your life or loss right now, what would it be? (Feel free to write down any lyrics that may be helpful to you.)

Baby Steps

Have you ever seen a baby take its first steps? They are usually tentative, cautious, small, and often end with a tumble. What happens next is the most important part: they giggle or cry and then get up and try again.

Baby steps must be approached with patience and perseverance, or we may never find our stride. What if I told you that simply taking baby steps to care for your physical body is the next step on your journey toward thriving?

One of the things I learned since my mom died in 2008 is that when I practice self-care, I have a lot more energy to do some of the deeper emotional work required for recovery. If you have ever been sick, you can understand what I am talking about. When we are physically sick or in pain, it is hard to do much of anything but rest. I know that when

I don't feel well, the chances of my going out in the world, interacting with others, or doing any personal growth are slim to none.

When it comes to grief, we generally focus on mental and emotional health, and we often neglect the impact on the physical body. Subsequently, we fail to consider how the improvement of the state of the physical body can positively influence our ability to heal our mental and emotional being.

By starting with your physical body, you have clear actions that you can take to heal. You also create more space in your heart, mind, and soul to fully heal and thrive in your life. Be patient with yourself, as you would be with a baby, and take one little step at a time. If you fall down, allow yourself to feel silly or sad and then get up and try again.

Compassion In Action: If you don't know where to begin go back to the basics: breath, water, movement, nourishment, and nature. Visit www.laurajack.com/7days-tothriving to download 7 Days to Thriving After Loss.

Create from the Core

"Who are you?" said the Caterpillar. This was not an encouraging opening for a conversation. Alice replied, rather shyly, "I—I hardly know, sir, just at present—at least I know who I WAS when I got up this morning, but I think I must have been changed several times since then." —*Alice's Adventures in Wonderland* by Lewis Carroll

When we experience loss and change, we often feel confused about who we are now. This confusion can be quite uncomfortable, thus it is a good moment to remember that you are not alone. Being confused about your role in the world, your likes and dislikes, or your purpose can leave you feeling deflated, sullen, and insecure.

If you are open to a reframe, consider this: as a survivor of loss, you have a unique opportunity to be better than the old you. When we experience loss, there is a natural stripping-away process that happens. Just as the ground after a fire is the most fertile place for growth, our life after loss has the potential for a new beginning that we never thought possible. What matters most becomes clear, and we have the chance to be our most authentic, best self. We get the chance to thrive rather than merely survive. During this step of your journey, you are in discovery mode.

You want to get curious about who you are at your core. Once you begin connecting to that part of yourself, you're able to decide who you want to be as you move into your new beginning.

Compassion In Action: What did you enjoy doing when you were a kid? How do you like your eggs? Who are 3 people you enjoy being around? Look toward the end of the book to find more self-discovery questions.

Discover What Thriving Means to You

In this step, we discover your plan to begin thriving. While you may feel down, dark, or lost, the beauty of your being here now is that you get to choose how you proceed. And no matter how you are feeling right now, the fact that you are here tells me that you want to thrive.

The following paraphrases a teaching from the Grief Recovery Handbook. As powerful as it is, it may also ruffle your feathers. If we don't take responsibility for our feelings and our reaction, we begin to make the death or other loss responsible for how bad we feel, and as long as we believe that someone or something else is responsible, it is nearly impossible to thrive.

I am not saying for you to take responsibility for what happened to you; I am encouraging you to take responsibility for your reaction and response to what happened. What happens when we don't take responsibility is that we lose our power.

What we must do to thrive is take responsibility for our emotions and recognize that we are the ones with the power to choose how we feel. As humans, we have an amazing ability to recover from any circumstance.

In the eye-opening documentary Happy, we learn that 50% of our happiness is predetermined by genetics and only 10% is related to our circumstance in life. That means 40% of our happiness is within our control. I am not saying that you can't be sad or experience grief. On the contrary, I believe being sad and expressing your emotions is crucial and normal, and I want to empower you to know that you are not a victim of your circumstances, but rather the creator of your life.

Deciding to Thrive

"We are not meant to stay wounded. We are supposed to move through

our tragedies and challenges and to help each other move through the many painful episodes of our lives. By remaining stuck in the power of our wounds, we block our own transformation. We overlook the greater gifts inherent in our wounds—the strength to overcome them and the lessons that we are meant to receive through them. Wounds are the means through which we enter the hearts of other people. They are meant to teach us to become compassionate and wise."

—*Caroline Myss*

If the ABCs program seems like something you want to engage in further, please visit www.laurajack.com, let me know that you read *The Compassion Code*, and I will send you a coupon.

Now, in order to move toward thriving, you have to determine what thriving means to you. Thriving looks different for every person on Earth. How will you know that you are thriving in your life? Will you be singing in the shower again? Will you be at your ideal weight? Is it as simple as feeling more patient? Does it mean you are experiencing more financial success? Or is it your being more present with your family and friends?

The more specific we can be about what our *thrive* looks and feels like, the more likely we are going to be able to get there.

Remember that thriving, like compassion, is a practice. When you are thriving, life will not be perfect. Thriving means growth; it does not mean that you will never feel sad or down again. It means that there will be more balance, more choice, and more confidence when it comes to living the life you want.

Please visit www.laurajack.com/7daystothriving and download the 7 Days to Thriving Ebook to get you started on your journey to thriving.

A FINAL REMINDER

"Be kind whenever possible. It is always possible." —Dalai Lama

When you haven't slept much and your child calls out in the middle of the night, it can be hard to get up graciously, patiently, and willingly. Sometimes our tendency is to wake up frustrated or even angry that we are disturbed from our sleep. That poor little one doesn't always receive the best version of us—they only get what we have available in that moment.

As a new parent myself, I am faced with the reality that I am human and unable to be perfect for my little one, no matter how badly I wish I could be. Sometimes the most important people to practice compassion with (besides ourselves) are the people we live with and love, and yet often they are the most challenging people to be compassionate toward. Isn't life funny that way?

I know for me, it can be easier to give strangers the benefit of the doubt than for me to be kind to my own husband.

Because of my mom's sudden death and the large number of grieving people I support, I hear story after story about people who have lost children, spouses, parents, siblings, and pets. I hear stories of divorce and estrangement. I hear stories about long-term illness, paralysis, and memory loss. And sadly, the list goes on.

Just like anyone who experiences a devastating loss, I had to pick up the pieces of my life and figure it out again. Understanding and honoring my own loss, as well as having a deep appreciation and respect for other people's life experiences, allows me to find my way back to gratitude and compassion in a split second.

Let's return now to the crying baby. She is mine, and I am exhausted. The last thing I want to do is get up. Here's how I find compassion for my daughter. I ask myself, "If today were our last day together, how would I spend this time with her?" This may sound morbid, but the reality is that we don't ever know what's coming in this lifetime. We have no guarantees. And when we lose sight of our mortality, we run the risk of losing our appreciation for life and the people who matter most to us.

My dad is a financial advisor, and he always says, "Laura, you have to find a way to balance your spending between saving as if you'll live until you're ninety, and spending as if tomorrow were your last day." I have found that this philosophy translates in every area of life.

Plan for tomorrow and live for today.

And always be kind no matter what. You rarely regret being nice.

I invite you to ask yourself this question anytime you're having trouble with compassion: "How would I treat this situation, this person, or myself if today were my last or theirs?"

Our mortality is part of the grief experience, and it is part of the growth experience.

Please remember that we are not perfect, we are human. Compassion takes practice.

I am grateful that I no longer have to run away, be afraid, or say the wrong thing when people experience loss. I am grateful that I'm able to be a support for you. It is such a gift to not feel helpless when life happens, and I hope you walk away with more confidence to communicate compassionately, even in what is normally considered an uncomfortable situation.

Now that you have more tools, please use them. Practice compassion and know that you are on your way to saying the right thing when the wrong thing happens.

Afterword

Madisyn Taylor, author of *DailyOm: Inspirational Thoughts for a Happy, Healthy & Fulfilling Day*, wrote a beautiful piece on compassion that seemed like she was writing it just for this book.

Compassion is the ability to see the deep connectedness between ourselves and others. Moreover, true compassion recognizes that all the boundaries we perceive between ourselves and others are an illusion. When we first begin to practice compassion, this very deep level of understanding may elude us, but we can have faith that if we start where we are, we will eventually feel our way toward it. We move closer to it every time we see past our own self-concern to accommodate concern for others. And, as with any skill, our compassion grows most in the presence of difficulty.

We practice small acts of compassion every day, when our loved ones are short-tempered or another driver cuts us off in traffic. We extend our forgiveness by trying to understand their point of view; we know how it is to feel stressed out or irritable. The practice of compassion becomes more difficult when we find ourselves unable to understand the actions of the person who offends us. These are the situations that ask us to look more deeply into ourselves, into parts of our psyches that we may want to deny, parts that we have repressed because society has labeled them bad or wrong. For example, acts of violence are often well beyond anything we ourselves have perpetuated, so when we are on the receiving end of such acts, we are often at a loss. This is where the real potential for growth begins, because we are called to shine a light inside ourselves and take responsibility for what we have disowned. It is at this juncture that we have the opportunity to transform from within.

This can seem like a very tall order, but when life presents us with circumstances that require our compassion, no matter how difficult, we can trust that we are ready. We can call upon all the light we have cultivated so far, allowing it to lead the way into the darkest parts of our own hearts, connecting us to the hearts of others in the understanding that is true compassion.

* https://dailyom.com/

References

James, John W. and Friedman Russell. *The Grief Recovery Handbook: 20th Anniversary Expanded Edition*. New York: William Morrow, 2017.

Morgenstern, Stacey and Carey Peters. Holistic MBA. (accessed 1 Feb. 2013).

Neff, Kristen. *Self-Compassion: The Proven Power of Being Kind to Yourself*. New York: William Morrow, 2011.

Orloff, Judith. "The Health Benefits of Tears." PsychologyToday.com. https://www.psychologytoday.com/blog/emotional-freedom/201007/the-health-benefits-tears (accessed June 21, 2017).

Mertz, John. "A Mindful Difference: Respond vs React." ThinDifference.com. https://www.thindifference.com/2013/03/a-mindful-difference-respond-vs-react/ (accessed June 21, 2017).

Flower, J. "In the Mush". *Physician Executive*. 25 (1) (1999): 64–6.

Lancaster, PA. "Amish Grace and Forgiveness." http://lancasterpa.com/amish/amish-forgiveness/ (accessed June 21, 2017).

Cope, David. R. "Freedom from Suffering: Feeling Feelings." DavidRCope.com http://www.davidrcope.com/davids-writings/freedom-from-suffering-feeling-feelings/ (accessed June 21, 2017).

Winch, Guy. "Why we all need to practice emotional first aid." Ted.com.

https://www.ted.com/talks/guy_winch_the_case_for_emotional_hygiene (accessed June 21, 2017).

Study Questions for Discussion and Reflection

1) What is the difference between compassion and empathy?

2) What happens on either extreme of compassion?

3) How can self-criticism and self-doubt interfere with our reactions to other people?

4) Is being compassionate something you can improve? If so, how can you practice compassion is some small way this week?

5) Can practicing self-compassion help strengthen self-confidence because we begin to alter the self-talk in our heads?

6) What are the steps we can use to build self-compassion? Does the pursuit of self-esteem interfere or complement this journey?

7) How do strong negative emotions and judgments affect you? How can they be modified?

8) What is the difference between forgiving and condoning?

9) Does having compassion justify hurtful behavior? What is the goal of having compassion in these circumstances?

10) Does how you feel about yourself really change how you react to others? How do you react to stress when you are tired, hungry, or bored? Does that change when you are relaxed and comfortable? What are some examples of this in your everyday life?

11) How can understanding the myths of grief impact how we deal with difficult emotional subjects moving forward?

12) An individual's experiences can profoundly modify their

perceptions. How can you increase your awareness of your map? What are some of the experiences that have greatly impacted your perspective?

13) What is a common scenario you experience that interferes with your compassion? How can you practice compassion in that situation?

14) What feelings do you experience when you read the section on how to have compassion for a killer? Are you thinking about justice or vengeance?

Uncover Your Story to Improve Self-Compassion (Continued from Chapter 5)

When, where, and how were you born?

How did you get your name?

What is your earliest memory?

Who are/were your parents?

Who are/were your grandparents?

Who were your primary caregivers growing up?

How did your family come to live where they did/do?

Do you have any siblings?

How do you relate to them if they are still living?

What are three happy memories from your childhood before you were 10?

What are three sad or painful memories before you were 10?

Who was your favorite person growing up?

Who did you relate to most?

Did you move before you were 15? What were those moves like?

When was the first time or a significant time that you were picked on or teased?

When is a time that you picked on someone else?

When was your first crush? Who was the person and how did you know him/her?

Who was your favorite teacher? What made them so special to you?

Who was your least favorite teacher? What was it about them?

Did you have any pets? If so, did you have to care for them?

What activity were you most challenged by?

What activity did you excel at?

What is one of your favorite summer memories from childhood?

Did you ever build anything?

Who was a mentor for you growing up?

Who, if anyone, were you scared of?

When was your first kiss? Was it good or bad?

When did you have your first boyfriend or girlfriend? How did it end, if it ended?

Were you ever put into a situation sexually that made you uncomfortable?

What was your favorite subject in school?

What was your least favorite subject in school?

What was a time where someone else was proud of you?

When was a time that you were proud of yourself?

What was a time where you disappointed someone you cared about?

What was a time where someone you cared about disappointed you?

When were you proud of where you come from?

When were you embarrassed of where you come from?

What was your religious upbringing? Did you like it or did you wish it were different?

What did you study (college, trade school, first job)?

What did you want to study if it wasn't the same as above? Did you follow through? If not, what happened?

What was your first job? How was your boss? How long did you work there?

What has your favorite job been? What made it your favorite?

What was your least favorite job? Why?

What is your favorite place you have ever lived?

Where do you dream of living that you haven't lived before? What is it about that place?

If you are married or in a partnership, how did you meet your significant other? When did you know you wanted to be with them?

Who is someone you miss?

What is your favorite thing to do in your free time?

What do you wish you could do more of?

Where is your favorite place you have visited?

What is a song that fills your heart with joy?

What is a song that brings you back in time?

What is a song that brings tears to your eyes?

What is your favorite book right now?

What was your favorite book when you were little?

Do you have any pets now? If so, what are their names and what do you love about them? If not, do you ever want any?

Do you have any children? If so, tell me about them. How old are they? What are they good at? What is something about them that you see in yourself? What is something that fascinates you about them?

What is something that annoys you?

Extra Resources for Mental Health Concerns

If you or someone you care about is in need of additional support, please seek professional help from a primary care physician, mental health professional, psychiatrist, or Grief Recovery Specialist. If you have serious concerns for someone's well-being (or your own), call 911 or utilize the resources below.

National Suicide Prevention Lifeline:

https://suicidepreventionlifeline.org/ or call

1-800-273-8255

Crisis Text Line: http://www.crisistextline.org is the only 24/7, nationwide crisis-intervention text-message hotline.

Samaritans: http://www.samaritansusa.org is a registered charity aimed at providing emotional support to anyone in distress or at risk of suicide in the United States.

Mental Health America: Information on mental health, getting help, and taking action. www.mentalhealthamerica.net

National Empowerment Center: Message of recovery, empowerment, hope, and healing to those diagnosed with mental illness. www.power2u.org

Mental Health First Aid: A national program to teach the skills to respond to preserving life when a person may be a danger to self or others, provide help to prevent the problem from becoming more serious, promote and enhance recovery, and provide comfort and support. https://www.mentalhealthfirstaid.org/

ASIST: https://www.livingworks.net/programs/asist/ Applied Suicide Intervention Skills Training (ASIST) is a two-day interactive workshop in suicide first aid. ASIST teaches participants to recognize when someone may have thoughts of suicide and work with them to create a plan that will support their immediate safety.

Self-Help Resources

If you want to continue on your own healing journey, please check out the resources below. I have found all of these helpful on my journey.

Axe, Dr. Josh. *Real Food Diet Cookbook*. Exodus Health Center, 2010.

Beck, Martha. *Finding Your Own North Star: Claiming the Life You Were Meant to Live*. New York: Harmony, 2002.

Bridges, William. *Transitions: Making Sense of Life's Changes*. DaCapo Press, 2004.

Cloud, Dr. Henry and Dr. John Townsend. *Boundaries: When to Say Yes, When to Say No to Take Control of Your Life*. Zondervan, 1992.

Crowe, Kelsey, PhD and Emily McDowell. *There Is No Good Card for This: What to Say and Do When Life Is Scary, Awful, and Unfair to People You Love*. New York: HarperOne, 2017.

Friedman, Russell and John W. James. *Moving On: Dump Your Relationship Baggage and Make Room for the Love of Your Life*. M. Evans & Company, 2006.

Grayson, Kaneisha. *Be Your Own Boyfriend: Decide to Be Happy, Unleash Your Sexy, and Change Your Life*. Amazon, 2013.

Hay, Louise. *You Can Heal Your Life*. Hay House, 1984.

Hendricks, Gay, PhD. *The Big Leap: Conquer Your Hidden Fear and Take Life to the Next Level*. New York: HarperOne, 2010.

Hendrix, Harville, PhD. *Getting the Love You Want: A Guide for Couples*. Henry Holt and Co., 2007.

Hickman, Martha Whitmore. *Healing After Loss: Daily Meditations for Working Through Grief*. New York: William Morrow, 1994.

James, John W. and Russell Friedman. *The Grief Recovery Handbook,*

20th Anniversary Expanded Edition: The Action Program for Moving Beyond Death, Divorce, and Other Losses including Health, Career, and Faith. New York: William Morrow, 2017.

James, John W. and Russell Friedman. *When Children Grieve: For Adults to Help Children Deal with Death, Divorce, Pet Loss, Moving, and Other Losses.* New York: Harper Perennial, 2002.

Katie, Byron and Stephen Mitchell. *Loving What Is: Four Questions That Can Change Your Life.* Three Rivers Press, 2003.

Rasmussen, Christina. *Second Firsts: Live, Laugh, and Love Again.* Hay House, Inc., 2013.

Ravikant, Kamal. *Love Yourself Like Your Life Depends On It.* CreateSpace, 2012.

Sandberg, Sheryl and Adam Grant, Ph.D. *Option B: Facing Adversity, Building Resilience, and Finding Joy.* New York: Knopf, 2017.

These are websites of people whose work has inspired me.

http://brenebrown.com/

Dr. Brené Brown is a research professor at the University of Houston Graduate College of Social Work. She has spent the past thirteen years studying vulnerability, courage, worthiness, and shame. Brené is the author of *Rising Strong, Daring Greatly,* and *The Gifts of Imperfection.*

http://thework.com/en

Byron Katie, founder of The Work, has one job: to teach people how to end their own suffering. As she guides people through the powerful process of inquiry she calls The Work, they find that their stressful beliefs—about life, other people, or themselves—radically shift and their lives are changed forever.

https://www.griefrecoverymethod.com/

The Action Program for Moving Beyond Death, Divorce, and Other Losses including Health, Career, and Faith.

http://www.secondfirsts.com/

Christina Rasmussen believes that when you experience a loss, a death, a divorce, a professional disaster, or any kind of devastating disappointment, it can be an experience that either shatters you forever, or an experience that inspires you to live, love, and create more fiercely than ever.

http://self-compassion.org/

Kristin Neff, Ph.D. is widely recognized as one of the world's leading experts on self-compassion. In addition to her pioneering research into self-compassion, she has developed an eight-week program to teach self-compassion skills in daily life.

http://juliesantiago.com/

Julie Santiago is a former Wall Street trader turned writer, speaker, teacher, and guide for women. She helps spiritual seekers discover who they are and why they're here so they can confidently share their gifts with the world.

http://www.shaynamahoney.com/

Shayna gives women hope to embrace their anxiety and find purpose and peace within by applying holistic health practices.

http://alchemyofhealing.com/causes-of-symptoms-according-to-louise-hay/

Causes of symptoms according to Louise Hay is a good place to start if you are looking for healing. Illness, however mild or severe, is an indicator of your emotional state, caused by your thoughts and focus.

http://turningwithin.org

Kelvin Chin is an international stress management and meditation expert. Kelvin learned to meditate at age nineteen, and has been teaching meditation in living rooms, schools, and businesses worldwide—and through FaceTime, Skype, and webinars—for forty-four years.

Acknowledgments

This book has been growing inside me for years. Sometimes projects live in our head and our heart, but never actually find their way onto the page. This book may have been one of those projects without the people who acted as my "book doulas."

A big thank you to Suzanne Boothby, my book coach and initial editor. Suzanne is a writer herself, and she understands how challenging it is to birth a book. She helped me get out of my own way and was patient with me when I felt stuck, scared, or incapable. She continued pushing me and believing in me even when I wasn't sure myself. Thank you, Suzanne, for reminding me that I am enough and that my words were helpful to you. At one point she said, "Imagine the thousands of Suzannes who will benefit from your book."

I also want to thank my dear friend Jackie Vecchio for helping with the organization of my book. Her ability to take a step back and organize my work in a way that made me excited to read it again was remarkable. Thank you, Jackie, for knowing me and my voice so well that you could help me create exactly what I wanted.

A huge amount of gratitude for David Schiff, Julie Santiago, Sharon Hymes, Daniel Saxe, Mor Regev, Heather Jernigan, Kaneisha Grayson, and Dayde McLaughlin for your expertise, insights, and editing collaboration. I could not have done it without you.

Thank you to my husband, Aaron, who constantly encourages me to grow and holds a bigger vision for me than even I hold for myself. Thank you for believing in me and for pushing me to share my insights with the world. Without you, none of this would be possible.

Thank you to the Grief Recovery Institute for being my guide and believing in me enough to share what I have learned as a Certified Grief Recovery Specialist. Thank you to my mentors who helped me become the coach I am, and who continue helping me grow.

A special thank you to my parents and my brother who helped me become the woman I am. My mom nurtured my intuition and desire to build meaningful relationships. My dad taught me to believe I could do anything, always reminding me to live life in balance. Thank you to my brother, David, who shaped me more than he knows.

Thank you to everyone involved in the publication of this beautiful book. My publishing coach, Alexa Bigwarfe and her team. My cover designers, Michelle Fairbanks and Samantha Paris Estes. And special thanks to Stacey Aaronson for a final edit.

A huge amount of gratitude for all of my clients who have taught me so much about compassionate communication. Thank you for sharing your stories so openly with me.

About Laura

Laura Jack teaches about compassionate communication and how we can relate to one another more effectively during the challenging moments in life. Using practices of self-care and self-love, she helps people rediscover their light after loss. Laura's mission is to cultivate a culture of compassion, starting with self, and to create a better understanding of loss and its accompanying grief.

If you want to learn more, visit www.laurajack.com and join the Army of Compassion at https://www.facebook.com/groups/thearmyofcompassion/ to build bridges of compassion and understanding.

Made in the
USA
Monee, IL